BRITAIN

IN OLD PHOTOGRAPHS

BRITISH
BREWING

GAVIN D. SMITH

SUTTON PUBLISHI

Sutton Publishing Limited
Phoenix Mill · Thrupp · Stroud
Gloucestershire · GL5 2BU

First published 2004

Title page photograph: Capturing the youth market?

British Library Cataloguing in Publication Data
A catalogue record for this book is available from the British Library.

ISBN 0-7509-3376-3

Typeset in 10.5/13.5 Photina.
Typesetting and origination by
Sutton Publishing Limited.
Printed and bound in England by
J.H. Haynes & Co. Ltd, Sparkford.

Beer! Happy produce of our isle
Can sinewy strength impart,
And wearied with fatigue and toil
Can cheer each manly heart.

James Townley, 1751

'You can't be a real country unless you have a beer and an airline. It helps if you have some kind of a football team, or some nuclear weapons, but at the very least you need a beer.'

Frank Zappa

CONTENTS

'King's Ale' brewed by His Majesty King Edward VII, 22 February 1902, during a visit to Bass & Co in Burton upon Trent.

An intriguing photograph from September 1923. Four women pose with two giant bottles of Worthington India Pale Ale. The circumstances of the portrait are not known, though perhaps the women are brewery workers. All four are clearly dressed for the occasion, though curiously one is holding a cigarette despite posing for the photograph.

1

A Brief History
of British Brewing

A postcard advert for Marston's prize-winning bottled pale ale, 1912.

Brewing has come a long way since medieval times when ale was made by monks in monasteries and by 'ale wives' in their own kitchens. It is now a multi-national industry, worth billions of pounds a year, and it is often difficult to keep up with the pace of takeovers and mergers, and the consequent disappearance of old breweries and brand names.

According to Frederick W. Hackwood in *Inns, Ales and Drinking Customs of Old England* (1909), 'the brewing of ale, as the frescoes of its ancient temples have revealed, was a skilled industry in Egypt five thousand years ago, and the ancient city of Pelusium was as noted for its breweries as for its university. . . . Herodotus ascribes the first discovery of the art of brewing "barley-wine" to Isis, the wife of Osiris; and a beverage of this nature, perhaps made from wheat, barley, and honey, is mentioned by Xenophon, 401BC.'

Sacks of malt at Frederick Robinson Ltd's Unicorn Brewery, Stockport, 1990s.

The Babylonians encouraged the brewing of good beer by drowning any under-performing brewer in his own drink, and Brian Glover, in *Beer: An Illustrated History*, asserts that 'the first detailed mention of beer was made more than 5,000 years ago by the Sumerians, who lived in the fertile land between the Tigris and the Euphrates in the area now known as Iraq'.

While the people of the Mediterranean countries drank wine made from grapes, it was logical that in cooler climates, where cereals thrived and vines did not, beer would become a staple drink. In Norse mythology the spirits of those who had died in battle feasted in Valhalla, a mighty banqueting hall with 540 doors, in which Woden entertained the warriors for all time with a never-ending supply of strong ale. The Norsemen of 3,000 or more years ago would bury a pot of beer in a grave to sustain the corpse in the afterlife, and archaeological evidence shows that in at least one instance it was made with wheat, using myrtle, cranberries and bilberries for flavouring.

Filling the grist hopper, York Brewery, late 1990s.

In 77AD Pliny the Elder wrote in his *Naturalis Historia* that in Western Europe tribes produced an 'intoxicating drink from corn steeped in water', and beer-making was well established when the Romans arrived in Britain. The wine-drinking Romans were unimpressed by it, however; Emperor Julian declared of English beer, 'who made you and from what, by the true Bacchus, I know not. He smells of nectar, but you smell of goat.'

By the medieval period, the brewing of beer was widespread throughout much of Europe. It was a much safer drink than water, with very little risk of infection, and consequently, a weak 'table beer' became the everyday drink for most people, with stronger brews being produced for festivals and other special occasions. Increasingly, barley was the main cereal used in brewing, principally because it malted more effectively and more easily than wheat or oats, and produced greater quantities of sugar to convert into alcohol.

Monasteries were hotbeds of brewing, and a network of such ecclesiastical centres spread throughout Europe from the fifth century onwards. Ale was brewed not only to serve the needs of the monks themselves, but also to sell to passing travellers and pilgrims, though the monks could certainly hold their own when it came to ale

A fermenting vessel in use at T&R Theakston Ltd's Masham Brewery, 1980s.

consumption. Burton Abbey, founded in 1004 by Wulfric Spot, Earl of Mercia, allowed its monks a daily ration of one gallon of strong ale, often supplemented by a gallon of weak ale.

It is sometimes maintained that the 'X' symbol, which persists to this day in beers such as Nimmo's XXXX, St Austell's XXXX Mild, and Wadworth's 6X from Devizes, was first used by monastic brewers as a pledge of good ale. The makers swore on the cross that the beer was of high quality, and the earliest barrel crosses were close to crucifixes in shape. Other sources say that the X originated in barrel marks applied by members of the Guild of Coopers, or that the X denoted beer on which 10s duty per cask had to be paid. 'XX' meant a beer that was twice as strong and therefore liable to twice the duty, and so on. If this version is true, the practice can only date from 1643 or later, as the first tax was imposed on ale in that year at an initial rate of 2s 6d per barrel.

Before the introduction of hops into England, ground-ivy and costmary were used to give brews additional flavour, while, according to Dr Plot's 1686 *History of Staffordshire*, 'About Shenstone [near Lichfield] they frequently use Erica vulgaris heath, or Ling, instead of Hopps, to preserve their beer, which gave it no ill taste.' It is recorded that hops were being cultivated in Hallertau, Germany, in 736AD, and in 1079 Abbess Hildegard of St Ruprechtsberg wrote that the plant, 'when put in ale, stops putrefaction and lends longer durability'.

The hop-vine probably appeared in England during the reign of King Henry VI (1422–61), being imported either by Kentish merchants or Flemish immigrants. It was widely disapproved of, being considered an adulterant, and the monarch banned its use by brewers. It was more than a century later that Henry VIII repealed the prohibition, and eventually the improvement to the flavour and longevity of beer imparted by hops became widely acknowledged.

Frederick Hackwood writes that, 'as to the interchangeable terms "ale" and "beer", it may be observed that in olden times beer was considered the superior variety of ale, and usually sold at twice its price; whereas nowadays at Burton upon Trent and many other places the classification is reversed. In former times beer was the stronger liquor, because it was the brew from the first mashing of the malt. The term "beer" was used by the Anglo-Saxons, but seems to have fallen into desuetude until the name was revived to distinguish ale from hopped ale. At the present day, while the term ale does not apply to porter or stout, beer embraces all kinds of malt liquors.'

It is difficult to be certain just when brewing developed into an organised, secular, commercial activity, but the sixteenth-century chronicler John Stow wrote that in 1414, 'one William Murle, a rich bruer and maltman of Dunstable, had two horses all trapped with gold', which suggests that there were enticing profits to be made from ale even in the early fifteenth century. Further evidence of the establishment of brewing as a substantial industry is supplied by the fact that in 1445 brewers were granted their first royal charter of incorporation by King Henry VI, which formalised a long-standing trade guild.

The eighteenth century saw a great increase in the size of breweries in large towns and cities. The population of Britain was increasing and more people lived in urban environments; with gin officially demonised, beer was promoted as a healthier alternative. Beer drinkers were also seen to be supporting British agriculture, and demand for the product grew rapidly.

The development of canals during the eighteenth century, and railways during the mid-nineteenth century, made transporting casks of beer much easier, cheaper and more worthwhile. Additionally, new technology, such as the steam engine, was embraced by major breweries. Whitbread installed a steam engine in its Chiswell Street Brewery in London in 1785 in order to pump water and grind malt, and twenty-four horses were rendered surplus to requirements by its introduction.

A cooper at work, T&R Theakston Ltd's Masham Brewery, 1920s/30s.

With growth also came greater experimentation and knowledge of the chemistry behind the brewing processes. Even during the nineteenth century there was still a great deal of ignorance regarding fermentation and the work of yeast. Louis Pasteur's visit to Whitbread's Chiswell Street Brewery in 1871, when he demonstrated the use of the microscope to analyse yeast, was a breakthrough for the industry.

During the eighteenth century, many London brewers in particular became men of substance and social acceptance. They were involved in politics and many other businesses, including banking. Brewing could be highly profitable, and Dr Samuel Johnson is recorded as saying in 1773 that the brewer Henry Thrale 'paid 20,000*l* [pounds] a year to the revenue, and that he had four vats, each of which held 1,600 barrels, above a thousand hogsheads'.

When Thrale died in 1781, the brewery was sold by Johnson and his fellow executors on behalf of Mrs Hester Thrale for the sum of £135,000. At the time, brewing was going through a boom period, and Johnson famously declared, 'we are not to sell a parcel of boilers and vats, but the potentiality of growing rich beyond the dream of avarice'.

The staff of Jennings Brothers' Castle Brewery, Cockermouth, mid-1990s.

The prosperity of London brewers was largely dependent on the popularity of porter, a mixture of three existing types of beer, reputedly developed by Ralph Harwood of the Bell Brewery in Shoreditch during the early 1720s. It was a great success with London's market porters, hence the name. Almost black in colour, porter was well-hopped and strong in character. The production of porter became the preserve of the largest and most affluent London brewing companies, as the investment in plant was considerable, and capital was tied up for comparatively long periods before a return was forthcoming due to the lengthy maturation times for the product. Brewers who were already established on a substantial scale, such as Whitbread, Truman and Barclay, tended to be best positioned to cash in on the porter revolution. Brewed in vast vessels, porter was effectively a traditional mild ale with a higher level of hopping than usual, and was matured for several months in very

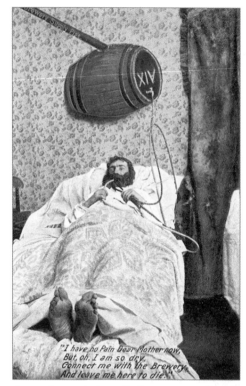

A popular early twentieth-century postcard.

large vats to increase its strength. Relatively new beer was 'blended' with much older beer before sale. The result was a beer that kept well and was comparatively cheap, owing to the large scale on which it was produced.

The popularity of porter only diminished during the nineteenth century as paler ales became more fashionable. East India Pale Ale was probably developed by Abbot & Hodgson of the Bow Brewery, and was comparatively light, sparkling and heavily hopped. It soon became a great success with middle- and upper-class drinkers in domestic markets and with British 'ex-pats' in India. It was first exported by the East India Company, hence its name. Just as London had been the porter capital of Britain, so Burton upon Trent developed into the country's principal home of pale ale production (see Chapter 4).

Many major brewers whose names were to become synonymous with British beer for more than two centuries set up in business during the eighteenth-century brewing boom. They included Allsopp, Bass, Charrington, Courage, Guinness, Meux, Whitbread, Worthington and Younger. Additionally, long-surviving regional brewers, such as Brain in Cardiff, Hall & Woodhouse in Dorset and Belhaven in Dunbar, were founded at this time.

John Courage began brewing at Horselydown, Southwark, close to the River Thames in 1787, having moved south from his Aberdeen birthplace eight years

The general office at Davenport's Brewery, Birmingham, mid-1930s.

previously. At the time, brewing was one of Southwark's major industries, and Courage grew to become one of the biggest and best-known brewing companies in England, making many acquisitions along the way before finally losing its independence to Imperial Tobacco in 1972.

Samuel Whitbread became the foremost brewer in eighteenth-century England. He was immensely wealthy by the time of his death in 1796, when he was the sole proprietor of what had become the most famous brewery in the world. Whitbread was born in 1720 in a Bedfordshire village, and at the age of sixteen was apprenticed to a brewer in Clerkenwell. In 1742 he entered into a partnership with Godfrey and Thomas Shewell, and during the late 1740s, Whitbread, with Thomas Shewell, built a new, large porter brewery in Chiswell Street.

In 1748 London brewers produced a staggering 915,000 barrels of porter, of which the twelve leading breweries contributed 383,000 barrels. Whitbread saw the way the industry was going and wanted to be a part of it. According to Berry Ritchie in *An Uncommon Brewer – The Story of Whitbread*, 'By the end of his life, Samuel Whitbread's Chiswell Street Brewery was one of the wonders of London, a staggering production and distribution complex filled with the very latest steam-powered technology, visited by royalty, and famous throughout the land.'

In 1758 Whitbread brewed some 65,000 barrels of beer, making it the largest producer of porter in London, and a decade later, the firm began to bottle beers, having seen Bass and Worthington bottled beers being imported from Burton upon Trent to the capital by rail. In 1796 Whitbread had the distinction of being the first brewer in the world to produce in excess of 200,000 barrels in one year.

The company became as well known during the twentieth century for its pale ales as it had been during the eighteenth for its porters. Even during the late nineteenth century, Whitbread was already expanding by acquiring existing brewing operations which it absorbed into its empire. This process was, in fact, more widespread than is generally realised. It is easy to think of consolidation within the brewing industry as an essentially post-Second World War phenomenon, but in reality many of the smaller rivals bought up by larger brewers during the later decades of the nineteenth century were summarily shut down.

During the middle of the nineteenth century, beer consumption stood at an astonishing 22 gallons per person per year, or nearly half a pint per day for every man, woman and child. There was an apparently ever-increasing growth in demand, and by 1900 production in Britain was around 40 million barrels per annum. Despite this, however, brewery numbers declined, with economic recession in the years before the First World War precipitating more amalgamations and closures. The situation worsened during the First World War as the Defence of the Realm Act curtailed public house opening hours. This move was ostensibly intended to curb drunkenness in areas of munitions production, but Chancellor of the Exchequer David Lloyd George was a noted anti-drinker, and this was a perfect excuse to rein in the brewers and distillers. 'Drink is causing more damage in the war than all the German submarines put together', declared Lloyd George. High levels of taxation on beer also conspired to shut breweries, and from the 6,477 still operating in 1900, fewer than 600 remained by the outbreak of the Second World War.

With a reduction of beer-drinking in licensed premises, the market for bottled beer was developed as a crucial way of creating a new market in the home, and the 1930s also saw greater emphasis on advertising and the development of innovative products such as canned beers.

Mergers, takeovers and brewery closures continued apace after the Second World War, when industry consolidation was at

A beer mat from Border Breweries (Wrexham) Ltd, 1970s.

The prince of Ales

BORDER

its most intense. For example, Joshua Tetley & Son Ltd merged with Walker Cain Ltd of Warrington in 1960 to form Tetley Walker Ltd, but the following year the new company joined forces with Ansells Ltd of Birmingham and Ind Coope of Burton upon Trent, ultimately trading as Allied Breweries Ltd and then as Allied-Lyons plc. In 1992 Allied was taken over by Carlsberg Breweries A/S of Copenhagen, and the wholly owned subsidiary Carlsberg-Tetley Brewing Ltd was created. Today it operates just two breweries in Britain.

By the late 1970s, six large organisations controlled much of Britain's brewing industry, the 'Big Six' comprising Allied, Bass Charrington, Courage, Scottish & Newcastle, Watney Mann & Truman, and Whitbread. More than thirty years later, of those six, only Scottish & Newcastle – with a near 30 per cent share of the British beer market – continues to have a brewing presence in the country. US company Coors and Belgian-based Interbrew are now two of Britain's other largest brewers.

Lochside Pale Ale bottle label, 1950s.

Two phenomena of the last couple of decades have been the rise of non-brewing 'pubcos' as owners of large estates of licensed premises, and the withdrawal of companies such as Whitbread and Bass from the ranks of the country's brewers (see Chapter 5).

Consolidation meant not only the loss of many familiar names, but also a trend from the 1960s onwards for national, and ultimately international, brands, with flavour and character often playing second fiddle to marketing conformity and mass-production convenience. Comparatively bland, processed and pasteurised keg beer rapidly began to replace cask ale, accompanied by the growth of the 'lager phenomenon'.

The Campaign for Real Ale (CAMRA) was formed in 1971 to fight for the survival of cask ale, and it has developed into a notably effective consumer pressure group, attracting in excess of 50,000 members. It has been successful in persuading some major brewers that 'real ale' remains worth producing, as well as encouraging the formation of many new micro-breweries, which offer a welcome return to localised, personal, responsive brewing of a wide variety of characterful beers (see Chapter 4 and Chapter 5).

2

Brewing Beer

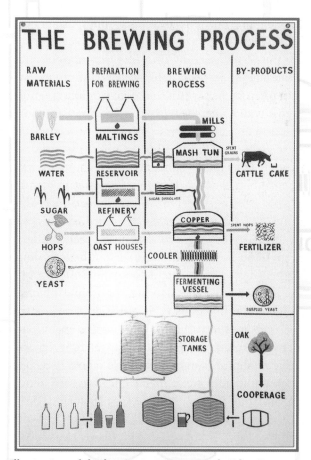

Illustration of the brewing process, Castle Eden Brewery,
County Durham, 1980s.

In order to produce beer a brewer requires four principal ingredients, namely barley, hops, water and yeast. The same basic principles apply whether he is brewing in a vast, modern automated brewery turning out thousands of barrels per week for international markets, or in a micro-brewery producing half a dozen casks for a couple of local bars.

Firstly, the barley must be malted in order to induce germination. In traditional floor maltings, the grain is soaked in steeps before being spread on a germinating floor at a depth of up to 9 inches. It remains there for some five days until germination has started, and during that time it is turned with wooden shovels to maintain an even temperature and humidity level. Once partial germination has occurred, the process must be arrested, or the newly developed fermentable sugars will be consumed by the growing plant. Germination is halted by baking the green malt (as it is known) in a kiln for around two days. This also has the advantage of imparting nutty, crunchy, malt flavours that will ultimately influence the flavour of the beer produced, as well as its colour.

Floor maltings are now operated only in a small number of breweries, as they are labour-intensive, vulnerable to seasonal temperature variations, and take up a great deal of space that can often be better utilised. Today, malting tends to be undertaken for brewers by specialist companies, using highly mechanised equipment designed to maximise throughput and minimise labour.

Once the malt arrives at the brewery it is milled to produce grist, which is subsequently mixed with hot water – usually referred to as liquor. This mixture is then pumped into mash tuns, where the grist yields a fermentable sugary, malty solution, known as raw wort or sweet wort. Any remaining sugar is extracted by spraying hot water onto the mash – a process described as sparging.

The sweet wort is transferred into the copper or brew-kettle, where it is boiled with hops for in excess of an hour. Some hops are put into the copper at the start of the process, while others are added later during the boil to give a final distinctive aroma. The length of the boil will also influence the strength of the final beer.

Boiling extracts the bitter flavours of the oils and resins in the hops which contribute to flavour and aroma, serves to sterilise the wort, and prevents further enzyme activity. There are many different varieties of hops, giving a wide range of aroma and flavour permutations. Some brewers use whole hop cones, lightly crushed before addition, though many now prefer their hops processed into pelletised form.

Once the boiling phase is over, the wort is transferred through a hop-back, essentially a filter to remove the hops and a vessel that has given its name to a brewery in Wiltshire. The wort is subsequently cooled, usually in heat exchangers, from where it is pumped to the fermentation vessels. There yeast is added, and the action of the yeast turns the sugars in the wort into alcohol and carbon dioxide.

After fermentation the green beer is transferred to conditioning tanks to settle and mature. The period of time it is left there depends on the style of beer being produced. A mild ale, for example, will require a shorter conditioning period than a lager. Indeed, bottom-fermenting beers such as lagers can spend weeks or even months in cold temperatures, as fermentation continues in the vessel.

The process of lager brewing was developed by Bavarian monks, who stored beer in cold cellars in order to see if this would increase its longevity. At lower temperatures the yeast sank to the bottom of the fermentation vessels rather than frothed on the surface. On the bottom, the yeast fermented more slowly, and the lager could, indeed, be kept for comparatively long periods of time.

Cask ales and ales for bottle-conditioning – beers where secondary fermentation takes place in the bottle – are neither filtered nor processed, but are simply racked into casks, or bottles, as they stand. Finings are added to many beers to give them clarity when dispensed, and dry hops may be used to impart extra aroma.

Pasteurisation of beers is commonplace, whether they are to be presented in keg, can or bottled form. This increases the life of the beer, and makes it more stable during storage. However, the yeast is killed along with bacteria, and the flavour is often thought to be adversely affected. Whereas the head on cask ale is a natural product of the brewing process, keg beers are artificially carbonated to ensure a creamy head at the point of dispensation.

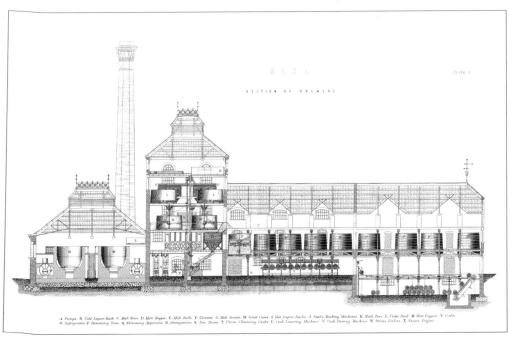

A sectional drawing of a brewery, 1890s. This is an example of a traditional tower brewery, in which the initial ingredients are either hoisted or pumped to the top of the tower, from where they progress by the force of gravity between each successive stage of brewing.

The Brake spring, St Austell Brewery, Cornwall, *c.* 2000. First used in 1912, this spring provides all the brewing water or 'liquor' needed by St Austell. Brewing requires a guaranteed supply of water, and its chemical composition is also of great importance. The salts that predominate in any particular sample of water can affect the quality and style of beer brewed. For example, excessive sulphate will give a sharp, bitter character, while too high a level of bicarbonate will make a mash that is unacceptably acidic, leading to inefficient sugar extraction from the malt.

Barley. Malt is largely responsible for the dominant flavours and colour in beer, and while cereals such as wheat and oats may be used, barley gives the most favourable extraction of sugars, hence its use as the principal grain in beer-making and whisky-distilling. The brewer, like the distiller, requires barley with a low nitrogen level because too much nitrogen can adversely affect fermentation.

Barley harvest, Bury St Edmunds, 1940s. To commemorate the return of brewery workers from the First World War, local brewers Greene King opened the Victory Sports Ground in the Suffolk town in 1926. This photograph was taken during the Second World War, when the land had temporarily reverted to agricultural use. The site is still a sports ground today, and is run by St Edmundsbury Borough Council.

A hop field at Queen Court Farm, Faversham, Kent, late 1940s. Queen Court Farm was acquired by Shepherd Neame Ltd in 1944 in order to secure a supply of quality hops for brewing. Medieval monasteries in central Europe probably first used hops for brewing, and it is recorded that beer made using hops was imported into the Sussex port of Winchelsea in 1400. Soon afterwards, Flemish brewers began to arrive in England, and made hopped beer just as they had at home. Most settled in and around London, and found conditions in Kent ideal for the cultivation of the plant.

A handful of hops. The hop plant – *Humulus Lupulus* in Latin – is a tall, climbing vine of the hemp family containing alpha acids, which give the hop its bitterness. It has roots that can be up to 6 feet in length, and requires sun to ripen. Traditionally, therefore, hops have been grown in the southern counties of England, and Scottish beer was usually brewed without the addition of hops at all. Even today, the more traditional styles of Scottish beer tend to be sweeter and less bitter than those from the south of England.

Below: The 'hop room', John Davenport & Sons' Brewery Ltd, Birmingham, early 1930s. Hops are harvested after the plants have flowered, and it is the cones that contain the alpha acids, in an oil called lupulin. Today, harvesting is largely mechanised, but until comparatively recently, it was work undertaken by the urban poor, often from the East End of London. The hop-pickers took their annual holidays in Kent, living in huts and tents for the duration of their stay. The introduction of a hop-picking machine in 1934 led to the demise of this tradition.

Hops in a cooling loft, Boughton, Kent, *c.* 1909. Once harvested, hops were dried in oasthouses, spread out on the floor of the drying room which was located above the kiln. The distinctive, conical roof of the oasthouse, with its characteristic cowl, was necessary in order to create a good draught to make the fire draw well. After heating, the hops were transferred to a cooling floor or loft adjacent to the drying room. Once cooled, they were packed or baled ready for delivery to merchants or direct to breweries.

Loading sacks of hops, Kent, *c.* 1906. Popular British brewers' hops include Goldings, which was developed in Kent during the eighteenth century and is ideally suited for dry-hopping ale in the cask, giving it a flowery bouquet. Fuggles is another long-established Kentish hop, developed by Richard Fuggle in 1875. At the height of Kent's hop-growing popularity, more than 30,000 acres of land in the county were dedicated to its cultivation.

Hardy's old malt kilns, Hardys & Hansons plc, Kimberley Brewery, Nottingham. The maltings were used until 1973 when malt began to be bought in from dedicated maltsters.

Traditional floor maltings at Jennings Brothers' Castle Brewery, Cockermouth, in use until the 1980s. The maltings have now been converted into company offices. The soaked barley is being turned to maintain constant levels of temperature and humidity and to prevent the developing rootlets from matting together.

Above: Sacks of malt in the malt room, Davenport's Brewery, Birmingham, early 1930s. Essentially, the higher the kilning temperatures of malt, the darker the colour and the fuller the flavour. Brewers usually blend different malts in their beers, and the principal types include Pale Malt, which is commonly used in light-coloured beers, and Crystal Malt, which is the result of rapid heating. It gives beer a sweet, comparatively full flavour. Chocolate Malt is heated to very high temperatures and has deep, roasted flavours and a dark colour which it imparts to beers in which it is used.

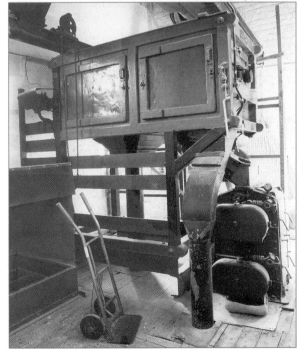

The milling machine, Jennings Brothers' Castle Brewery, Cockermouth, 1990s. The milling machine grinds the malt in order to crack open every grain so that it will be fully exposed to the action of the liquor, or hot water, during mashing. The ground malt is known as grist.

A wooden mash tun, Shepherd Neame's Faversham Brewery, 1946.

Bill Epps cleaning the wooden mash tun at Shepherd Neame's Faversham Brewery, 1946, after the wort has been run off and the spent grains removed for use as cattle feed.

Victorian mash tuns at Young & Co's Ram Brewery, Wandsworth, London, *c.* 1929. These mash tuns remained in use until 1977.

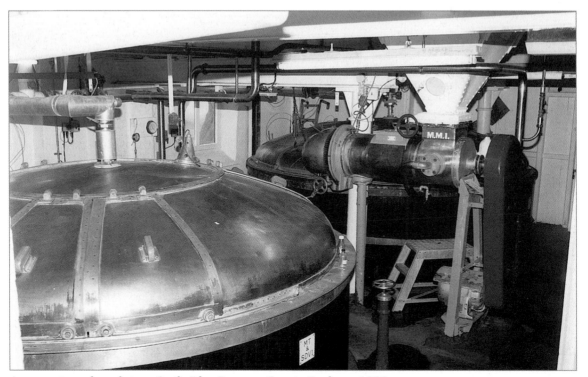

A copper-topped mash tun, Castle Eden Brewery, County Durham, 1980s.

Above: The Victorian coppers at Young & Co's Ram Brewery, photographed in about 1929. They were used until the early 1980s.

An open copper, dating from about 1900, still in use at Hardys & Hansons' Brewery, Kimberley, Nottingham, in 1982, when this photograph was taken. Here wort is being collected before boiling with hops.

A brewing copper, Castle Eden Brewery, 1980s. Although the term copper continues to be used, modern coppers – sometimes known as kettles – are actually constructed from stainless steel, which is much easier to keep clean.

A modern brewing copper at Jennings Brothers' Castle Brewery, Cockermouth, 2003. The copper is located in the new brewhouse which was opened in July 1985 by celebrated Cumbria-based mountaineer Chris Bonington.

Foreman Bill Wise attends the wort coolers in the brewery room at Shepherd Neame's Faversham Brewery, 1940s. The hot wort is cooled by heat transfer until it is at a suitable temperature for yeast to be added. The warm water produced in the coolers is utilised in the next brew.

Slate squares at the Ram Brewery, Wandsworth, *c.* 1929. Although now covered with stainless steel, they continue in everyday use. In the *CAMRA Dictionary of Beer*, Brian Glover defines a square as 'a particular traditional form of fermenting vessel of a square shape, formerly made of stone or slate slabs, although new ones are stainless steel. The top is partially covered in, with a central hole to allow the escape of yeast and carbon dioxide. Especially common in the north, they are often known as Yorkshire Squares.'

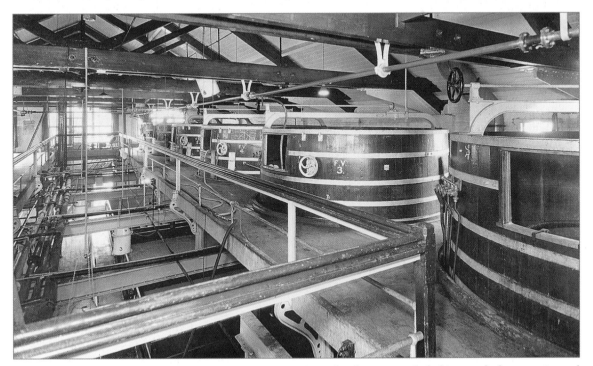

Cylindrical fermenting vessels, the Ram Brewery, *c.* 1929. Made of copper and clad in wood, they are situated on the floor above the slate squares. Although slightly modified, these vessels also remain in regular use.

A traditional, copper-lined, wooden fermenting vessel, Castle Eden, 1980s.

The union room, Allsopp's Brewery, Burton upon Trent, early twentieth century. The unique union system of fermentation was developed in Burton during the nineteenth century. Fermentation begins in shallow open vessels, but after a short time the liquid is pumped into a row of joined wooden casks. The activity of yeast and carbon dioxide force the liquid out of the casks and up swan-neck pipes into the barm troughs above the casks. The yeast remains there, while the liquid flows back into the casks. A very clear beer with a distinctive character is the result. Today, only Marston's continues to use the union system (see p. 82).

Installing one of seven 480-barrel fermenters at
Shepherd Neame's Faversham Brewery, 1985.
This addition greatly augmented capacity and
enabled the brewery to increase its lager
production. Four outdoor fermenters were
installed in 1995 to extend capacity by another
2,000 barrels. Enclosed vessels allow for more
precise control of fermentation and reduce the
risk of contamination.

Lifting a fermentation
vessel into Everard's newly
constructed Castle Acres
Brewery, Leicester,
c. 1984. The new brewery
replaced the Tiger
Brewery in Burton
(see p. 83), which finally
ceased producing Everard's
ales in 1990. In that year,
Castle Acres' capacity
was increased to nearly
70,000 barrels per
annum. Everards Brewery
Ltd remains an
independent family firm,
run by the great-great-
grandson of William
Everard, who founded the
company in 1849.

'Pitching' yeast, Whitbread & Co's Chiswell Street Brewery, London, 1950s. As soon as the yeast is added to the wort in the fermenting vessel it starts to multiply, and by the time the fermentation stage is at an end, there will be as much as five times more yeast than there was at the start of the process. The yeast's multiplication uses up all the oxygen in the wort, after which the yeast cells convert fermentable sugars to ethanol and carbon dioxide, along with a variety of minor chemical compounds.

Below: Skimming yeast during fermentation, Greene King's Westgate Brewery, Bury St Edmunds, Suffolk, probably 1950s. Surplus yeast forms a head and is skimmed off the surface of the wort during the fermentation process, which lasts up to seven days for beer and at least ten for lager, with the former being fermented at a higher temperature than the latter. Yeast can work on the surface in top-fermented beers and at the bottom of the fermenting vessel in the case of bottom-fermented lagers. Every brewery has its own strain of yeast which influences the character of the finished product.

Above: Head brewer Arthur Willis inspects a sample of Everard's beer at the Trent Brewery in Burton upon Trent, 1920s. Between the wars, the Leicester-based firm of W. Everard & Co brewed a best mild, a bitter and a best bitter in Burton. It was not until after the Second World War that beer brand names came into vogue.

Young & Co's head brewer John Sprake tests beer clarity with the aid of a candle at the Ram Brewery, Wandsworth, late 1950s.

Above: More sophisticated methods of quality analysis are undertaken today, as may be seen in this 1990s photograph of the laboratory at St Austell Brewery in Cornwall.

Racking beer into wooden casks, Whitbread & Co's Chiswell Street Brewery, London, 1950s.

Above: An early cask-cleaning machine, Jennings Brothers' Castle Brewery, Cockermouth, pre-1914.

Cleaning casks the labour-intensive way at Theakston's Brewery, Masham, North Yorkshire, undated.

The various stages
of barrel-making,
1950s.

A cooper at work, T&R Theakston's Masham Brewery, North Yorkshire, *c.* 1920s. The coopering craft probably dates back to ancient Egypt, but today only a handful of coopers are still employed in British breweries. They make the wooden casks by hand after undertaking a four-year apprenticeship.

Initiation of a newly qualified cooper, T&R Theakston's Brewery, Masham, 1980s. The ceremony is known as trussing in. Spent yeast and hops are poured over the cooper after he has climbed into a hogshead of his own making. It is then rolled around the brewery yard.

Tarring and feathering an apprentice cooper at the end of his training, Fuller, Smith & Turner's Griffin Brewery, Chiswick, London, 1956.

Ranks of traditional wooden barrels at Jennings Brothers' Castle Brewery, Cockermouth, 1950s. Casks are invariably made from oak, and every brewery once had its own team of coopers, employed in making and repairing barrels. Beer brewed at Theakston's Masham brewery and at Sam Smith's Brewery in Tadcaster, North Yorkshire, is still filled into wooden casks. Both breweries continue to employ coopers.

Aluminium kegs, Boddington's Strangeways Brewery, Manchester, 1970s. The 1930s saw the introduction of casks made from stainless steel and aluminium. They have the advantages of being cheaper to make than wooden barrels, require no maintenance, and are lighter for draymen to manoeuvre. Traditionalists argue that, as with whisky, the beer can take on positive colour and flavour characteristics from wood.

Hansons Brewery bottling plant, Kimberley, Nottingham, *c.* 1929. In 1929 Hansons won the prestigious Brewing Trade Review Challenge Cup for the country's best bottled beer. The figure in the centre is foreman William Wilson. The equipment featured in the picture was for chilling the beer after it left the fermenting vessels and for bottling it.

Simonds' bottling hall employees, Reading, 1911. The company of H&G Simonds was founded in 1768, and the Broad Street Brewery featured in this photograph opened in 1783. The company was acquired by Courage Ltd in 1960, and during the 1970s the brewery moved to an edge-of-town site. Despite its modernity, however, it was closed in 1979 during a programme of company rationalisation.

Gladys Patchery washing and checking returned beer bottles at Shepherd Neame's Faversham Brewery, 1930s. The use of returned bottles persisted until 1991, when the bottle-washing machine was removed from the bottling line.

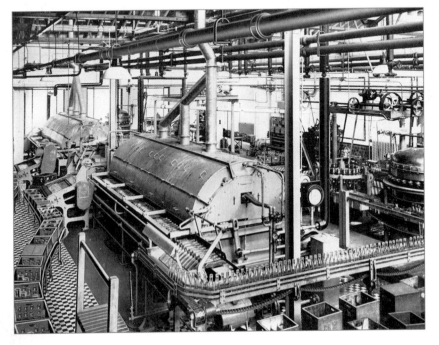

Bottle washing, Davenport's Brewery, Birmingham, early 1930s. Initially, hand-manufactured glass bottles were used for exported beers, having been developed during the seventeenth century, but the advent in the mid-nineteenth century of machinery to mass produce bottles, led to a great increase in the sale of beer in bottled formats. Steam-powered machinery also enabled bottles to be filled and crowned (or capped) much more easily, and brewers began to develop their own distinctive bottles.

Bottling line girls at Greene King's Westgate Brewery, Bury St Edmunds, 1939. Within days of the outbreak of the Second World War sixty of Greene King's male employees had joined the armed services. This left acute shortages of labour, and these two photographs show some of the women from Bury St Edmunds and surrounding villages who helped to keep the bottling line functioning through the war years. This was really nothing more than a return to old brewing practice. Frederick Hackwood notes that 'in early English times, when brewing was a domestic industry, the trade was entirely in the hands of women'.

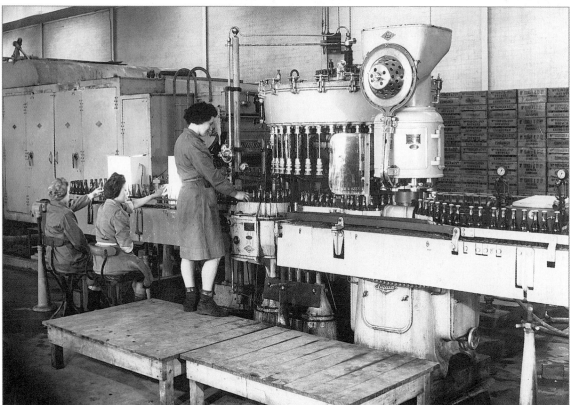

Women workers on the bottling line, Greene King's Westgate Brewery, Second World War. Before the development of machines to apply metal closures to beer bottles, they were corked, initially by hand and later by corking machines. A single worker could cork up to 350 bottles per day, but the corking machine installed by Whitbread & Co at its Chiswell Street Brewery in London during the 1890s could cork around 11,000 bottles per day.

Bottling and stoppering,
Davenport's Brewery, 1930s.
Early bottles were dark green or
brown in colour, but from the
early twentieth century clear
glass was often used, and the beer
thus presented had to appear
sparkling and appetising. It was
therefore usually chilled, filtered,
carbonated and pasteurised.
Bottling for the domestic market
steadily grew in importance
during the years following the
First World War.

Labelling bottles, Davenport's Brewery, early 1930s. Early beer bottles tended to be embossed with the company name, but the twentieth century saw the introduction of paper labels, which grew gradually more complex and professional in design and execution as time went on.

Crown corking machine, Whitbread & Co's Chiswell Street Brewery, London, 1950s. The metal crown cap was developed in the USA during the early 1890s. *The Licensed Victuallers' Year Book* for 1900 noted of the Ind Coope Brewery in Burton upon Trent that 'connected with this department [the bottling department] is a room used for bottling beer by machinery. These clever inventions do marvels, for they fill and cork no less than three dozen bottles of beer a minute – obviously a great saving of time and labour. They only require the attention of two pairs of hands to look after them, and perform wonders.'

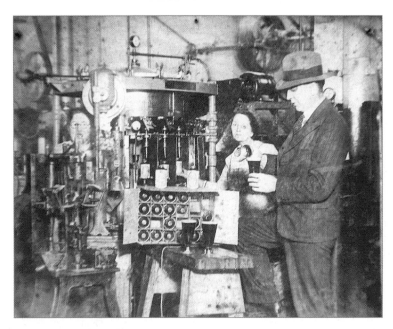

Felinfoel Brewery's head brewer Sidney John samples the first cans to come off the production line, December 1935. London's first canning factory had opened in 1812, and the canning of foodstuffs became a major business as the century progressed. A breakthrough in beer canning came in 1933 at the Gottfried Krueger Brewery in Newark, New Jersey, and by the end of 1937, no fewer than thirty-seven US breweries were canning beer. Britain was sceptical, but the tinplate industry of South Wales was in crisis and needed a new outlet; Felinfoel at Llanelli earned the distinction of being the first brewery in Europe to produce canned beer (see p. 94).

Office staff, Greene King's Westgate Brewery, Bury St Edmunds, 1958.

Opposite: Tennent's lager cans, 1970s. Following Felinfoel's successes, other British brewers soon became involved in the canning revolution, with Jeffrey's of Edinburgh, fellow Scottish brewers Tennent and McEwan, and London-based Perkins & Hammerton all rushing to can their own products. By the end of 1936 two million cans of beer had been produced in Britain, and by the autumn of the following year twenty-three British breweries were offering over forty canned brands. Tennent's became famous for presenting its lager in cans featuring glamorous young women – dubbed 'lager lovelies' – from 1962 onwards.

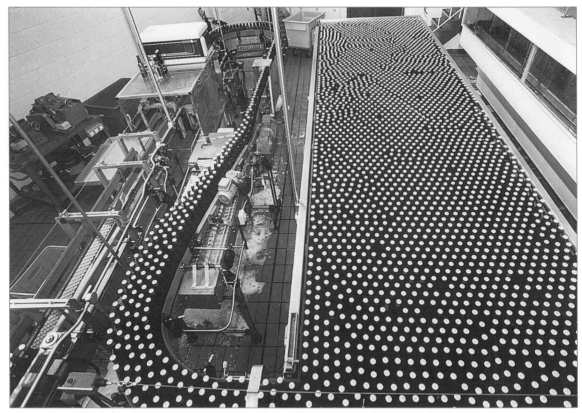

The new bottling line, Faversham Brewery, 1996. The line is fully automated with stainless steel bottle and pack conveyors and automatic labellers.

The control room of the Federation Brewery, Dunston, Tyne & Wear, 2001, with supervisor Bob Appleton on duty. All brewing operations have been controlled from this room since the brewing process was fully automated in 2000. Previous increases in capacity at the Federation's old Newcastle city centre brewery (see p. 102) had not been sufficient to meet demand, and in June 1980 this new state-of-the-art brewery costing £18 million was opened south of the River Tyne at Dunston. The new plant produces 500 barrels of beer every three hours, a far cry from the 500 barrels per week turned out in 1930.

3

Brewery Transport

The motorised fleet of Frederick Robinson Ltd, Stockport, Cheshire, *c*. 1920.

More photographs exist of brewery transport than of any other facet of British brewing. It seems that every time new horse-drawn wagons, steam engines or motor lorries were acquired, a photographer was summoned to capture them on film for posterity.

This is hardly surprising, because such vehicles were the public face of the brewery as they went about their business of delivering beer. Bearing a company's livery or the names of its most popular brands, they served as advertisements in addition to their primary, functional role. At its most extreme, this promotional aspect was reflected in vehicles such as Worthington's Daimler 'bottle car' (see p. 56).

For several centuries, brewing was comparatively localised, partly because poor transport links made it impossible for beer to be carried any great distances. However, as brewery mergers occurred during the nineteenth and twentieth centuries and small brewers were swallowed up by their bigger neighbours, beer had to be delivered across larger areas, and transport became more important than ever.

The 1935 book *Fifty Years of Progress*, which features John Davenport & Sons' Brewery Ltd in Birmingham, embraces many aspects of the company's operations. Space is devoted to the 'Motor Transport Fleet', and includes photographs of Davenport's 'spacious modern garage . . . a well organised and completely equipped repair shop, in which practically all types of repairs can be undertaken is an important feature of the Garage'.

When *The Licensed Victuallers' Year Book* correspondent visited Ind Coope's vast Romford Brewery thirty-five years earlier, however, he recorded that 'three hundred and seventy vehicles are used for delivery, and 543 horses'. Shires were the favoured breed of brewery horse, and were first used to pull drays during the eighteenth century. In 1800 it was reckoned that a leading London brewery would require fifty horses for every 100,000 barrels of beer it sold, and it is estimated that by 1900 some 150,000 horses were employed in drinks-related roles in Britain.

Although horse-powered brewery transport was superseded by steam and motor vehicles, some companies were notable for continuing their association with horse-drawn drays. They included Joshua Tetley & Son Ltd in Yorkshire and the London breweries of messrs Young and Fuller. Young & Co's Brewery still makes daily deliveries around Wandsworth using a pair of shires and a dray, and Frederick Robinson Ltd of Stockport in Cheshire also boasts a team of shires which deliver locally and attend shows and carnivals, proving a great attraction wherever they go.

Horses were still the principal source of motive power for breweries at the outbreak of the First World War, but many were commandeered by the army and few returned. After the war, motor vehicles became more readily available, and in many cases the switch to motorised fleets was soon made. In Burton upon Trent, for example, Bass & Co had around 200 horses in use in the late nineeenth century, but by 1921 that figure had fallen to 120, and just 36 remained a decade later.

Steam wagons were first used by the Guinness Brewery in Dublin in 1897, but by the early years of the twentieth century many other breweries had also embraced them. Records at the St Austell Brewery in Cornwall estimate the annual running costs in 1928 for its Foden steam wagon at £500, with £301 12s of that amount devoted to the wages of two men. Steam wagons were used for a comparatively short period, having been largely superseded by petrol-engine vehicles by the later 1930s. Many brewery photographs from the 1920s tend to show fleets of newly purchased motor vehicles, with a few steam wagons parked somewhat forlornly at the periphery. Open-backed petrol and diesel-powered motor wagons were used for several decades before being largely replaced during the 1980s by fully enclosed or 'Tautliner'-bodied vehicles for reasons of security.

Road transport was not, of course, the only way of moving beer from A to B. When the Young family's involvement with the Ram Brewery began in 1831, one attraction of the site was the fact that a canal from the River Thames had recently been excavated close to the brewery buildings. The canal basin could hold up to thirty barges, the principal means of heavy transport at the time, and the brewery utilised the canal for the supply of coal and malt.

John Cornish, head horse-keeper, in the stable yard at Young's Ram Brewery, Wandsworth, with two of his prize shires, 1930s. Cornish was the son of the brewery gardener and started work for the company in 1875 at the age of seventeen. He was employed in the stables for a remarkable sixty-seven years, dying at the age of eighty-four while still on the payroll. Deliveries of beer around Wandsworth continue to be made with a pair of shires and a dray, and Young's horses also have the high-profile role of pulling the Lord Mayor of London's carriage at the annual Lord Mayor's Show.

With the advent of steam trains, breweries had a new and comparatively swift means of obtaining coal, malt and other materials, and of dispatching casks of the finished product to their markets. The arrival of the railway in the Kent town of Faversham in 1858 allowed the company of Shepherd Neame & Co to extend its trade in the London area, and the brewery was soon expanded as a result. Major commercial growth of Burton upon Trent as a brewing centre followed the arrival in the town of the Midland Railway's Birmingham to Derby line in 1839. Previously, however, the Trent Navigation Act of 1712 had encouraged industrial expansion by allowing the transportation of beer and other commodities by narrow boat from Burton to the port of Hull. From there the beer was exported to Russian and Baltic ports, or shipped coast-wise to markets in London and Edinburgh. In 1777 the Trent & Mersey Canal System opened, linking Burton to Liverpool on the west coast, as well as to Hull on the east.

To capitalise upon railway developments, by the late nineteenth century Bass & Co had constructed 16 miles of private track in Burton, linking its various enterprises to the public railway network. On occasions, special trains were chartered to move beer, and during November 1897 the *National Guardian* reported the transportation of 350 hogsheads of Glenlivet ales from the Craigellachie Brewery on Speyside by special train to Aberdeen, en route to a customer in the south. According to the *National Guardian*, it took eighteen railway wagons to carry the consignment.

A journeyman delivering casks of beer by horse-drawn dray in Billingsgate Market, London, 1909. A journeyman was not a regular brewery employee, but was paid for work as required.

A St Austell Brewery dray delivering beer in St Ives, Cornwall, 1900. The brewery used a combination of horse-power and steam wagons from 1906 onwards, but the minutes of a meeting of directors in July 1923 noted the intention 'to purchase a two-ton and a five- or six-ton Leyland lorry. Horses to be disposed of as soon as big lorry is delivered.'

Fuller's dray and pair of shires, probably 1930s. Fuller, Smith & Turner bought their first steam lorries in 1903, and in 1936 these took over completely from the brewery's shires. In 1946 diesel lorries were purchased, and steam vehicles were phased out. Shires returned to the Griffin Brewery in 1989, however, when Griffin and Pride were acquired. They attend shows and make promotional appearances on behalf of the Chiswick-based brewing company.

Six open, horse-drawn drays and two fully laden, steam-powered drays about to leave Jennings Brothers' Castle Brewery, Cockermouth, to begin the day's deliveries before the First World War.

A Shepherd Neame & Co brewery traction engine disabled by a broken axle in East Street, Faversham, en route to collect fodder for the dray horses at Tankerton, 1914. The driver is Edwin Sims.

A heavily laden steam dray prepares to leave Jennings Brothers' Castle Brewery, Cockermouth, pre-First World War.

An aerial view of Young & Co's Ram Brewery, Wandsworth, *c.* 1930. Note the stable block in the centre and towards the rear of the photograph. The canal is behind. The canal had been created a century earlier, and it greatly enhanced the attractions of the brewery's location for Charles Allen Young and his partner Anthony Fothergill Bainbridge, who purchased it in 1831.

The barge *Centaur* moored alongside Harvey & Son's Bridge Wharf Brewery, Lewes, Sussex, late nineteenth century. Industry was attracted to the banks of the River Ouse at Lewes by the good communications afforded by barge transport. The brewery used barges to bring coal from Newhaven to fire the boilers and also to carry grain during the malting season. The arrival of the railway at Lewes during the 1840s reduced reliance on the canal, but barges continued to be used by the brewery until the early years of the twentieth century.

Motor delivery vehicles flanked by steam wagons, Felinfoel Brewery, Llanelli, Wales, 1920s.

The ultimate promotional brewery vehicle – a 1924 Daimler TL.30 'bottle car', originally purchased by Worthington & Co for £1,028, and one of five such vehicles operated by the company, which merged with Bass in 1926. It was photographed while on display at the Montagu Motor Museum during the 1950s. John Worthington founded a brewery in Burton upon Trent in 1774, three years before William Bass, and Worthington's India Pale Ale, as advertised on the 'bottle' and also known as White Shield, is now produced by the Museum Brewing Co in Burton.

A restored van originally used for local deliveries by the Masham brewery of T&R Theakston Ltd, photographed at the North Yorkshire brewery, 1980s.

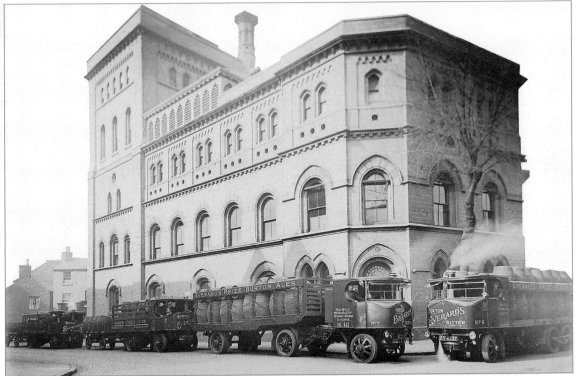

Steam wagons at W. Everard & Co Ltd's Southgate Street Brewery, Leicester, *c.* 1930. Everard's began to use steam-powered drays in 1924, employing them to carry beer from its Burton upon Trent brewery to Leicester. A transport inventory for 1924 lists two 6-ton and one 10-ton Super Sentinel articulated six-wheel steam lorries, along with two 5-ton Foden steam wagons, as well as five petrol lorries and three horse-drawn drays. The steam vehicles were considered to be economical and reliable, and continued in use until 1946, when petrol vehicles superseded them.

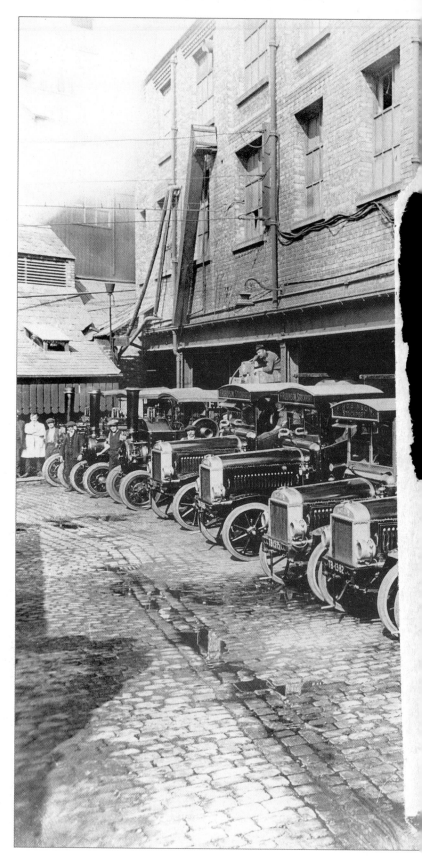

Robinson's fleet of Leyland drays at the Unicorn Brewery in Stockport, *c.* 1920. Three old steam wagons can be seen on the extreme left of the picture. In many cases, former stables were converted into garages when delivery fleets were mechanised.

A humorous depiction of a beer delivery, featuring the Bass 'red triangle' – first adopted in 1855. The trademark and company name became so ubiquitous that they appeared in many popular postcards of this type, published from the First World War onwards. This example dates from about 1950.

Part of John Davenport & Sons' motor transport fleet at the company's Bath Street premises, Birmingham, early 1930s. In 1935 the firm operated a transport fleet of 140 lorries of various sizes.

Davenport's home delivery of bottled beer, early 1930s. John Davenport & Sons' Brewery Ltd became famous for its 'beer at home' service, and was one of the earliest pioneers of deliveries to private addresses. This service commenced in 1904, to the vocal opposition of retailers and wholesalers alike. By 1939 the company had more than 250,000 customers who were supplied with beer from a network of regional depots.

More modern brewery transport at Jennings Brothers' Castle Brewery, Cockermouth, early 1980s, shortly before the entire fleet came to consist of fully enclosed delivery wagons. Note the miniature barrel on the open Bedford TK dray proclaiming the arrival of 'Real Beer'. Launched at the 1960 Motor Show, the Bedford TK range was a staple of the brewing industry until production ceased during the 1970s.

A long-distance Northern Clubs' Federation Brewery trailer with Leyland tractor unit pictured below the Tyne Bridge, Newcastle upon Tyne, 1980s.

4

Breweries of Britain

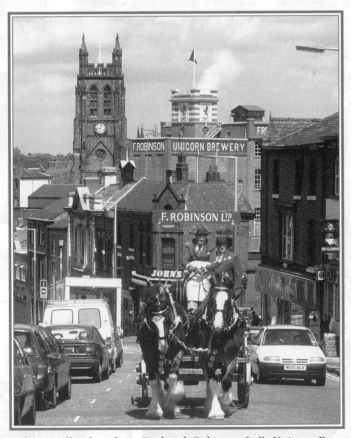

Two shires pull a dray from Frederick Robinson Ltd's Unicorn Brewery
through the streets of Stockport in Cheshire, with the brewery buildings in the
background, early 1990s.

Once British brewing moved away from its monastic and domestic roots and was established on a commercial scale, a number of locations became notable as brewing centres. They included London, Burton upon Trent and Edinburgh. Additionally, however, most towns and many villages had their own breweries during the nineteenth century, though as the century progressed many smaller brewers were taken over by larger operators – a process that has continued to the present day (see Chapter 1). By 1840 there were 50,000 breweries in Britain, but just forty years later that number had halved, and by 1900 fewer than 6,500 remained. When the Second World War broke out in 1939, the total had plummeted to under 600 and numbers continued to fall during the subsequent half century.

With so many breweries closing, new uses have been found for some of their redundant buildings. Retail and residential conversions have taken place in a number of cases, but many more have been demolished to make way for new developments. Sometimes, their very existence is recalled only by a 'Brewery Street' or 'Hop Lane' road sign.

London's concentration of population made it inevitable that the capital would develop a sizeable brewing industry, but in many instances the location of a brewery was dependent not just on local markets or good transport links, but on other crucial factors such as the availability of suitable brewing water. The water of Burton upon Trent in Staffordshire percolates through gypsum rock and small amounts of gypsum are dissolved as it does so. This makes it rich in calcium sulphate, and the sulphate ions are partly responsible for the characteristic bitter, dry taste of the classic Burton style of pale ales. The calcium ions aid the conversion of starch into sugar during mashing, and later in the brewing process also aid the precipitation of solids – which produces a sparkling, bright beer.

It was the monks of Burton Abbey (founded c. 1002) who first discovered that the local water was excellent for brewing, although they did not know why. According to *The Licensed Victuallers' Year Book* for 1900, Burton was a place 'where the tall red chimneys and massive brick buildings tower on all sides, and where across the roads steam modern locomotives in the town of John Barleycorn, [where] more than three hundred years ago our forefathers brewed the beer which has made the town on the banks of the silvery Trent famous throughout the universe'. The publication claimed that 'Burton ales . . . did not find their way to London until 1630, when they were sold at the Peacock, in Gray's Inn-road, and it was not until about 1748 that the beer was exported'.

It was during the eighteenth century that true commercial brewing was established in Burton. The first 'common' brewer is recorded as Benjamin Printon, who founded a brewery near Burton Bridge in 1708. There were nine breweries in

Burton in 1791, but at the height of the town's prosperity, more than thirty were turning out some three million barrels per annum in 1888.

Brewers in the south-east of England saw what was happening in Burton, and some decided that the best course of action was to set up their own brewing operations in the Staffordshire town. Ind Coope acquired a Burton base in 1856, then in 1872 Charrington & Co moved there. They were closely followed by fellow London brewers Truman, Mann, and Crossman & Paulin, all of whom established their own pale ale breweries. Many pale ale-producers outside Burton began to add gypsum salts to their water in order to replicate the 'Burton factor'.

By the middle of the sixteenth century there were twenty-six 'common brewers' in London, as well as the alehouse brewers who produced beer just for consumption on their own premises. As we have seen (Chapter 1), London became famous for its porter, and writing in the *Hand-Book of London* in 1850, Peter Cunningham declared that 'the Great Breweries are those of Barclay, Perkins, and Co, Park st, Southwark, Meux and Co, Tottenham Court Road, Combe, Delafield, and Co, Castle st, Long-acre, Whitbread and Co, Chiswell street, Truman, Hanbury, and Co, Brick Lane, Spitalfields, Goding and Co, Belvedere road, Lambeth, Reid and Co, Liquorpond st, Gray's Inn Lane, Calvert and Co, 89 Upper Thames st, Elliot and Co, Pimlico.'

Edinburgh's development into the second largest centre for brewing in Britain after Burton upon Trent was largely due to the quality of the water into which its brewers could tap. An underground lake – known as the 'charmed circle' – runs from Arthur's Seat to the Fountainbridge district of the city, with an offshoot running into Craigmillar, and breweries were gradually developed along much of its course. According to Marian McNeill in *The Scots Cellar*, 'The water contains a high percentage of gypsum, and it is this invaluable mineral element that constitutes the "magic" which has imparted to Edinburgh ales their distinctive quality down the centuries. . . . By the eighteenth century, the ales of Edinburgh had won a very high reputation.' The Scottish capital's hard, gypsum-rich water was ideal for pale ales, and thirty-six breweries were operating in Edinburgh by 1900. Twenty-three remained active during the 1930s, but today there are just two.

Against this backdrop of remorseless rationalisation and integration, the last couple of decades have witnessed a welcome growth in new small-scale breweries, producing characterful and imaginative beers. According to CAMRA's *Good Beer Guide 2004* there are in excess of 450 British breweries classified as 'independent', varying in scale from brew-pubs to major operators. What the *Good Beer Guide* classifies as 'global giants' operate some sixteen breweries in Britain at the time of writing. More than twenty new breweries had been set up since the 2003 edition of the annual publication appeared, but the 1997 edition recorded that a remarkable sixty-eight new breweries had been founded during the previous year.

The South of England

The south of England boasts an interesting mix of national, regional and micro-brewing operations, including a number of large-volume keg plants such as Diageo's Guinness Brewery at Park Royal in London and the ex-Bass Manor Park Brewery at Alton in Hampshire, now run by Coors Brewers Ltd. Long-established regionals include such well-known names as Young & Co's Brewery plc and Fuller, Smith & Turner plc in London, T.D. Ridley & Sons Ltd at Chelmsford in Essex, Harvey & Son (Lewes) Ltd of Sussex, and the Kent brewery of Shepherd Neame Ltd at Faversham. The St Austell Brewery Co Ltd remains the last large-scale commercial brewer in the West Country, though the micro-revolution of recent years means that a dozen or more small-scale breweries and brew-pubs now operate in Cornwall, with no fewer than seventeen in the neighbouring county of Devon at the latest count.

Young's Ram Brewery, Wandsworth, London, following a fire, May 1882.

Meux's Brewhouse, London, early nineteenth century. Meux's Brewery Co Ltd was based in Tottenham Court Road, where Henry Meux built the Horseshoe Brewery in 1810. In October 1814, a vat of maturing ale in the brewery burst, releasing some 320,000 gallons of liquid. The deluge smashed its way through the brewery wall and caused serious damage to many nearby properties. In total, twenty people died, some due to injuries caused during the flood of beer, while others were crushed to death as they tried to drink the free ale flowing through the streets. A few died as a result of alcoholic coma.

Barclay's Anchor Brewery, Southwark, London, 1829. The brewery was constructed on the site of the Globe Theatre, soon after its demolition in 1644. It was subsequently owned by the Thrale family, who were friends of Dr Samuel Johnson. After the death of Henry Thrale in 1781, the brewery was sold to David Barclay of the Quaker merchant family that founded Barclays Bank, and he went into partnership with John Perkins, the brewery manager. By 1815 the Anchor was the leading brewery in London, producing some 330,000 barrels of porter per year. Barclay, Perkins & Co merged with Courage Ltd in 1955.

'View of the brewery and dwelling house belonging to Messrs Calvert & co, erected on the site of Cold Harbour, 1820'. The brewery was located on the City bank of the Thames, just to the east of today's Blackfriars Bridge. The Calvert family were brewing during the second half of the seventeenth century, when London could boast 200 'common brewers', and this was one of London's dozen leading porter breweries by the early nineteenth century. In 1880 Calvert's was the sixth largest porter brewer in the capital, turning out some 200,000 barrels per year.

Porter racking room, Truman, Hanbury, Buxton & Co Ltd's brewery, c. 1900. The brewery was built at Lotsworth Field, Spittlehope, in 1669 by Thomas Bucknall, and The Licensed Victuallers' Year Book for 1900 described it as 'one of the greatest and most prosperous breweries in the world', noting that 'the porter fermenting tun no. 67 is known as the "Last of the Mohicans". . . . During the exhibitions of 1851 some North American Indians did their war dance in this immense vat, which holds 1,400 barrels.'

A group of employees at Fuller, Smith & Turner's Griffin Brewery, Chiswick, *c.* 1900. The Thames-side Griffin Brewery has been in existence for more than 350 years, and the firm of Fuller, Smith & Turner was founded in 1845. John Fuller had joined the brewery in 1829, and descendants of the original partners are still actively involved in running the business. In 1889 a hot air balloon bearing the slogan 'Fuller's Beers of Honest Repute' was purchased and was often to be seen floating above the brewery and at sporting and agricultural events.

The aftermath of a fire at Young & Co's Ram Brewery, Wandsworth, May 1882. Although the damage was extensive, business continued almost as usual, with the firm buying in beer from other breweries to supply its customers while a new brewhouse was being constructed. A report from *The Times* newspaper for Sunday 14 May 1882 noted that 'the fire gained such a mastery that it was not extinguished for 3 hours and a half after the first discovery of the outbreak, by which time the whole of the buildings were completely gutted and machinery destroyed'. One copper, in use since 1869, survived the fire.

The brewery yard, Ram Brewery, 1896. There was a brewery in this location during the reign of Queen Elizabeth I, and it is reputedly the oldest site in Britain on which beer has been continuously brewed. Young's is noted for its high-quality cask ales, and today Young's Bitter is the firm's leading draught ale, while speciality beers such as the distinctive honey-flavoured Waggledance have a devoted following. Family involvement is still very much the order of the day at the Ram, and Young & Co's Brewery plc is one of London's two remaining full-scale independent breweries, the other being Fuller, Smith & Turner plc.

Opposite: The original Old Star Brewery at Romford, nineteenth century. According to *The Licensed Victuallers' Year Book,* by 1900 the Romford Brewery had become 'the largest family brewery in the world. . . . During twelve months the quantity of beer sent out was 12,634,016 gallons. The wages paid amounted to £84,810. The brewery gives employment to 588 men and 154 boys. . . . Three hundred and seventy vehicles are used for delivery, and 543 horses.' The brewery operated until 1992, latterly under the auspices of Allied, and was demolished in 1998 to make way for a mixed retail, leisure and residential development.

Edward Ind. In 1799 the Star Inn in Romford, with a thriving brewhouse attached, was purchased by Mr Edward Ind and a Mr J. Grosvenor. Grosvenor was subsequently replaced as a partner by John Smith. Then in 1845 Smith sold his share to Mr O.E. Coope, whose brother also became involved, and the firm ultimately became known as Ind Coope & Co.

T.D. Ridley & Sons Ltd's Hartford End Brewery, Chelmsford, Essex, 1990s. Thomas Dixon Ridley (b. 1814) ran his father's milling business at Hartford End, and in 1841 married Lydia Wells, who came from a Chelmsford brewing family. Within a year Ridley had built a brewery on the banks of the River Chelmer, downstream from the family mill. Ridley's remains proudly independent and trades as 'The Essex Brewer'. In 2002 the company acquired the Tolly Cobbold brands and estate, and now brews Tolly Original and Tolly Mild, in addition to its own core cask ale brands such as IPA, Old Bob, Prospect and Rumpus.

Rayment's brewery appeal postcard, 1987. The reverse of the card features an appeal to Greene King & Sons plc managing director Simon Redman to reconsider the company's decision to close Rayment's brewery, which it had purchased in 1931: 'Rayment's drinkers should be allowed to continue enjoying BBA brewed at Furneaux Pelham.' The closure of the small Hertfordshire brewery of Rayment & Co Ltd in 1987 brought to an end 137 years of brewing tradition. Subsequently, the site was developed for residential use, which involved the conversion of brewery buildings and an oasthouse.

A seaside postcard featuring Watney's beers, mid-1950s. By this time the name of Watney's had become as ubiquitous as that of Bass (see p. 60). Until its closure in 1959, Watney & Co ran the Stag Brewery in London's Pimlico, which had been in existence for more than 300 years. Subsequently, the Stag's production was transferred to the Mortlake Brewery. Watney's was once synonymous with its Red Barrel beer, the *bête noire* of the 'real ale' movement, but today the name of Watney and its most famous product have disappeared, swallowed up in a labyrinthine series of takeovers.

Harvey & Son's Bridge Wharf Brewery, Lewes, Sussex, early twentieth century. In 1833 the Lewes brewer John Harvey purchased the Bridge Wharf Brewery for £3,707, and in 1881 the brewery was completely rebuilt. The Victorian Gothic-style buildings remain today, though a doubling in size of the brewhouse in 1985 and a subsequent increase in fermentation capacity mean that the independent family brewer can now produce in excess of 34,000 barrels per year. Harvey & Son Ltd is known for its fine range of cask ales, which include Sussex Mild Ale, Pale Ale, Best Bitter and XXXX Old Ale.

Bill Epps observing wort flowing into a fermenting vessel, Shepherd Neame's Court Street Brewery, Faversham, 1940s. Shepherd Neame Ltd is the only surviving full-scale independent brewer in Kent, and two teak mash tuns dating from 1910 remain in use, though in 2000 £2.2 million was spent on a new brewhouse which gives the company a capacity of 200,000 barrels per year. Shepherd Neame is best known for its Spitfire Bitter and the curiously branded Bishop's Finger. This beer takes its name from the unusual, finger-shaped signposts unique to Kent that were once used to guide pilgrims on their way to Canterbury.

Percy Beale Neame, who joined the Faversham brewing firm of Shepherd & Mares in 1864. He became sole proprietor of what was subsequently Shepherd Neame & Co in 1877. Brewing had taken place in what is now Faversham before the Great Abbey was built in 1147, and there was excellent local spring water and abundant supplies of high-quality barley. The brewery is believed to have been founded on the present site by Captain Richard Marsh in 1698, though records show that brewing was taking place there during the twelfth century.

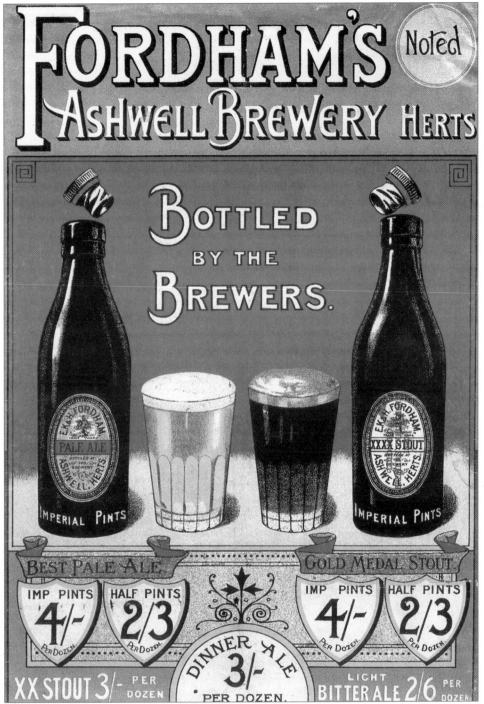

An Ashwell Brewery advert, undated. The Ashwell Brewery of E.K. & H. Fordham Ltd in North Hertfordshire was established in 1855. The village of Ashwell grew up around the springs that form the River Rhee, a tributary of the Cam, and this water source influenced the brewery's location. Fordham's owned an estate of 124 public houses, and the company survived as an independent entity until 1952 when it was taken over by the J.W. Green Group of Luton. The Ashwell Brewery became a bottling plant for Green before its closure in 1965. Flats were subsequently built on the site.

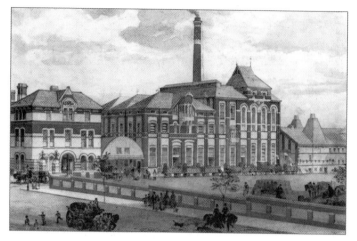

The newly completed Dorchester Brewery, Dorset, 1881. The Dorchester Brewery was owned and operated until 1997 by Eldridge, Pope & Co plc, a company whose origins go back to 1837. In 1870 the brewery came under the control of the Pope family, and with Alfred Pope at the helm the business expanded dramatically. In 1881 the new brewery opened alongside the London South-Western Railway line, and in 1890 it produced 44,326 barrels of beer, more than four times the capacity of its predecessor. This was the largest brewery in the South-West, but brewing ceased in 2003.

Brewery staff and float, St Austell Carnival, 1949. St Austell Brewery was founded by Walter Hicks, who set up in business as a maltster in 1851, and Hicks's great-great-grandson, James Staughton, has been managing director of the proudly independent St Austell Brewery Co Ltd since 2000. All 150 of St Austell's pubs offer cask ales, and the range includes the popular Tinner's Ale, Dartmoor Best Bitter and Tribute. Although expansions have taken place over the years, the heart of the present brewery remains the original plant which opened in 1893.

The Midlands, East, West & Wales

T he Midlands were once the heartland of the British brewing industry, and today large-scale, high-volume breweries are operated by Coors Brewers Ltd in Burton upon Trent and Carlsberg-Tetley Brewing Ltd at its dedicated lager plant in Northampton. In Wales, Interbrew UK Ltd runs The Brewery at Magor in Monmouthshire, formerly owned by Whitbread, while the other major Welsh brewers are the independent duo of S.A. Brain & Company Ltd in Cardiff and the Llanelli-based Felinfoel Brewery Co Ltd. In the east of England, George Bateman & Son Ltd of Lincolnshire and the Suffolk duo of Adnams plc and Greene King plc fly the flag for established regional brewers with rich histories behind their names. In Burton upon Trent no fewer than five micro-breweries have emerged to carry on the proud tradition of beer-making alongside their surviving larger neighbours.

Bass Brewery's Middle Yard, Burton upon Trent, 1934. William Bass was born in Hinckley, Leicestershire, and ran a carrier business, establishing himself on the outskirts of Burton. He probably chose the location because it was half-way between Manchester and London, the two principal cities with which much of his trade was conducted. Burton was also becoming increasingly industrialised and there were large quantities of locally brewed beer for Bass to carry. In 1777 Bass purchased a house on the town's High Street with a modest brewery attached, and the story of one of Britain's greatest brewing companies began.

Ind Coope's Burton Brewery, 1899. In 1856 Ind Coope & Co set up a brewery in the burgeoning brewing centre of Burton upon Trent, and according to *The Licensed Victuallers' Year Book* for 1900, 'in the brewery tower there are five floors. . . . No. 2 fermenting room is one of the finest, if not the finest in Burton. It contains twenty-eight oak rounds, polished and brass-bound, whilst the interiors are copper lined and tinned over. These rounds have a capacity of 95 barrels each, so the total gallons would be 93,600, or just upon two million glasses of bitter, and this is only one room.'

Ind Coope's Burton Brewery, 1899. For many decades, Bass and Ind Coope were the two undisputed Burton brewing giants, until Ind Coope – by then part of Carlsberg-Tetley – sold its Burton plant to Bass in 1998 after Bass's plans to merge with Carlsberg-Tetley were blocked by the government. In the summer of 2000 Belgium-based Interbrew acquired the Bass brewing operation, and the following year Coors purchased four Bass breweries and the Shobnall Maltings at Burton for £1.2 billion. Interbrew retained the Bass breweries in Belfast and Glasgow, along with the Tennent's lager and Bass ale brands.

E. Jesser Coope. According to *The Licensed Victuallers' Year Book* for 1900, 'he was born in 1850, educated at Eton and Christchurch, Oxford, joined the firm of Ind Coope & Co. in the year 1873, where he was more particularly attached to the Burton branch, managing the export department. . . . Of late years he has devoted almost the whole of his time to yachting, and has been to all the principal places in the world on his yacht *Sunrise*. At the present moment [1900] he is en route to Durban with doctors and nurses in aid of our wounded in the present [Boer] war.'

An aerial view of the Trent Brewery, Burton upon Trent, probably 1930s.

Bass's Dixie Ale Bank, Burton upon Trent, 1930s. Michael Thomas Bass, grandson of the company's founder, inherited a small provincial brewery turning out 10,000 barrels per year, but the arrival of the railway in Burton in 1829 provided the impetus for expansion, and by the 1880s Bass had built two new breweries in the town which gave an annual output of almost one million barrels. The company's three breweries employed a workforce of 2,500 at that time, with 1,300 staff in the engineers' department alone. During the 1880s, the Bass stave store, where timber associated with casks was kept, covered no less than 25 acres.

Samuel Allsopp & Sons' Brewery, High Street, Burton upon Trent, 1912. The business was originally formed by Benjamin Wilson and in 1807 was acquired by Samuel Allsopp. By the early 1900s the company was in serious financial trouble and it went into receivership in 1913. In 1934 it merged with Ind Coope & Co to form Ind Coope & Allsopp Ltd. Allsopp's had expanded dramatically from Wilson's original site, and the old brewery was rebuilt in the 1840s, with a new brewery being constructed during the late 1850s. In 1899 the old brewery (pictured) was taken out of mothballs and converted to lager production.

Marston's Brewery, Burton upon Trent, early twentieth century. The company of Marston, Thomson & Evershed has been part of Wolverhampton & Dudley Breweries plc since 1999, but the firm's origins in Burton date back to 1834. Marston's is the last brewery to use the Burton union system of fermentation (see p. 30), and the company claims that the oak casks of the union system produce a unique variety of yeast that gives beers like the famous Pedigree Bitter its distinctive character. In 2003 the brewery on Shobnall Road received a £1.7 million investment, and plant from the decommissioned Mansfield Brewery was installed to help keep pace with demand.

Burton Bridge Brewery, Burton upon Trent, late nineteenth century. The Leicester brewing company of Everard, Son & Welldon leased the Bridge Brewery, Umplett Green Island, Burton, from 1892 in order to meet growing demand for its beers. The Bridge had been established in 1865 and was owned by Henry Boddington & Co Ltd. It had an annual capacity of more than 10,000 barrels, but this was not sufficient for Everard, who gave up the lease and moved to the nearby Trent Brewery in 1898.

The Trent Brewery, Burton upon Trent, undated. The Trent Brewery was built in 1881 by the Liverpool brewer Thomas Sykes, but in 1886 the Trent Brewery Co went into liquidation. Two years later W. Everard & Co leased the brewery, buying the freehold in 1891 for £9,000. The firm subsequently renamed it the Tiger Brewery, and ran it in tandem with the Southgate Street Brewery in Leicester until the closure of that plant in 1931.

Bass & Co's workers and their families disembarking from a train at Burton railway station after one of the firm's famous annual outings, c. 1900. Between 1865 and 1914 Bass treated its workforce to excursions, latterly on an annual basis. Blackpool, Great Yarmouth, Scarborough and Liverpool were the usual destinations, and in 1900 no fewer than 11,241 employees and their families travelled to Blackpool on a total of seventeen trains. The locomotive in the photograph is numbered '12'. Each workman was allocated 2s 6d spending money in addition to his usual daily wage, while foremen were given 5s.

Brunt Bucknall Brewery, Woodville, *c*. 1906. The brewery, seen on the right-hand side of the High Street in this photograph, was established in 1832 by Charles Brunt and Samuel Bucknall. The brewers' trademark was a six-pointed star. When the business was registered as a limited company in 1890 with a capital of £60,000 in £10 shares, it boasted 49 freehold pubs and 46 leasehold establishments. Annual output was between 20,000 and 28,000 barrels. In 1919 the company was taken over by Salt's Brewery of Burton upon Trent, which in turn was absorbed by Bass in 1927. Both breweries were subsequently closed.

Hinckley Road Brewery (extreme right), Hinckley, Leicestershire, early twentieth century. There is an old rhyme that goes 'Higham-on-the-Hill, Stoke in the Dale, Wykin for butter, Hinckley for ale', and in *Leicestershire* (1809) Nichols mentions the existence in Hinckley of an ale and porter brewery run by Francis Ward.

Above: Mitchell & Butler's Cape Hill Brewery, Smethwick, Birmingham, 1930s. The brewery was founded in 1878, and in its first year of production employed 271 people and produced 90,000 barrels of beer. Between 1912 and 1914 a second brewery was constructed, capable of producing a further 30,000 barrels per week. In 1961 Mitchell & Butler Ltd merged with Bass, and its identity was gradually submerged in the vast Bass Charrington empire. In 1994 Bass opened a £60 million redevelopment of the site, but following the sale of Bass assets to Coors, the brewery closed in 2002 and 320 employees lost their jobs.

An aerial view of John Davenport & Sons' Brewery Ltd, Bath Row, Birmingham, early 1930s. The firm had its origins in 1739, but the imposing Bath Row brewery was opened in 1896. Davenport's was taken over by Greenall Whitley & Co Ltd in 1986, along with an estate of 123 pubs, and the brewery was closed three years later. The Davenport brands were produced at Shipstone's Brewery in Nottingham for a while by Greenall Whitley until it ceased brewing and became a purely retail operation in 1990. Today, the Bath Row brewery site has been transformed into student accommodation.

Hansons Brewery, Kimberley, Nottingham, after completion in 1895. Four gilded reproductions of the George III Golden Guinea top the brewhouse. Stephen Hanson established the original brewery in 1847, and for many years it stood on the opposite side of the road to its principal rival, Hardy's. The two companies amalgamated in 1930 and as Hansons was the smaller of the two it was chosen for closure, the last brew completed on 22 December 1922. The buildings were demolished in 1973.

Hardy's Brewery, c. 1895. Brothers William and Thomas Hardy took over Robinson's Brewery in Kimberley and proceeded to construct a new, enlarged brewery on the site in 1861. In 1922 Hardy's Brewery had a capacity of 1,000 barrels per week, and in 1933 that capacity was extended. Subsequent expansions have taken place, but the brewhouse in the centre foreground of the photograph is still working today. Members of the Hardy and Hanson families continue to serve as directors of the company.

Shipstone's Brewery dray in front of the Council House, Nottingham, undated. James Shipstone's Star Brewery in New Basford, Nottingham, was founded in 1852 and closed in 1991, having been acquired by Greenall Whitley in 1978. The author of *A Dictionary of Agriculture* (1726) wrote that 'the chief thing about Nottingham ale is in the making of it, which is only when 'tis working to let it stand in a tub four or five days before it is put into the cask; stirring it twice a day and beating down the head or yest into it, which gives it the sweet aleish taste'.

Ellis & Co's brewery, Drury Lane, Lincoln, undated. Ellis's brewery nestled below Lincoln's magnificent eleventh-century cathedral, which stands on Lincoln Edge. Today, the county's brewing heritage continues in a number of micro-breweries and the old-established family firm of George Bateman & Son Ltd at the Salem Bridge Brewery in Wainfleet. Bateman's was founded in 1874 and must surely be the only brewery in Britain to feature a full-scale windmill.

The Westgate Brewery fire brigade, Bury St Edmunds, undated. The risk of fire was great in breweries and as national fire services were limited in scope and ability, many brewers set up their own operations. The Westgate Brewery fire brigade was formed by Greene King in 1888 and was not disbanded until 1998.

An unusual and slightly sinister brewery advertising item – a clockwork king, photographed in 1949 when it was being used for promotional purposes by Greene King. Today, the company prides itself on its range of cask ales, being best known for Greene King IPA, Abbot Ale, Ruddles County Ale and the Morland duo of Hen's Tooth and Old Speckled Hen.

The present brewhouse under construction at Greene King's Westgate Brewery, Bury St Edmunds, 1938. Greene King plc is now Britain's largest regional brewer with an estate of 1,600 public houses spread across the south of England. CAMRA describes Greene King as a 'super regional', following its acquisition of the famous Ruddles and Morland brands. Ale has been produced in Bury St Edmunds since at least 1086 and Benjamin Greene began to brew in the historic town in 1799. He merged his venture with the St Edmunds Brewery of Frederick King in 1887.

The Theatre Royal barrel store, Bury St Edmunds, probably 1930s. Originally opened in 1819, the Theatre Royal stood opposite the Greene King brewhouse and was purchased by the brewery in 1920. The company struggled to keep it operating as a theatre and after a few years it closed, but the building was used as a barrel store from 1925 until the early 1960s. A group of local people subsequently raised funds to restore the old theatre, and it eventually reopened in 1965. The freehold is still owned by the brewing company, but the building was vested in the National Trust in 1975 on a 999-year lease.

Bell's Brewery, Hempshaw Lane, Stockport, early twentieth century. In 1949 the area's premier brewer, Frederick Robinson Ltd, acquired Bell's as it continued its programme of expansion. In 1915 Robinson's had purchased Heginbottom's Borough Brewery in Stalybridge, going on to acquire Scholfield's of Ashton-under-Lyne in 1926 and Kay's Atlas Brewery in Manchester three years later. Bell & Co Ltd had built a new brewery in 1930 and was the largest acquisition undertaken by Frederick Robinson Ltd. Robinson's position as the leading brewer in north Cheshire was confirmed by the purchase, and Bell's brewery continued in production until 1968.

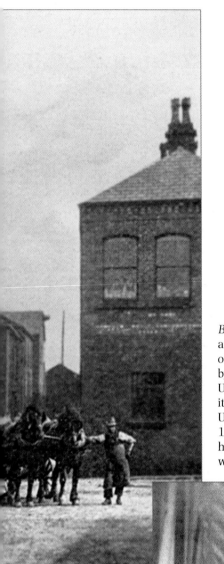

Below: Frederick Robinson and his wife Emma with their son William and daughter Mary, *c.* 1870. The North-West-based brewing company of Frederick Robinson Ltd was founded at the Unicorn Inn in Stockport by Frederick Robinson, whose descendants still run the business. The Unicorn Inn was built on Lower Hillgate in 1722, and within a decade it is recorded that John Warren was operating a brewhouse on the Unicorn site. William Robinson became landlord of the Unicorn in 1826, and in 1859 his son Frederick (pictured) took over the inn from his elder brother, George, and expanded the brewhouse into a wholesale operation.

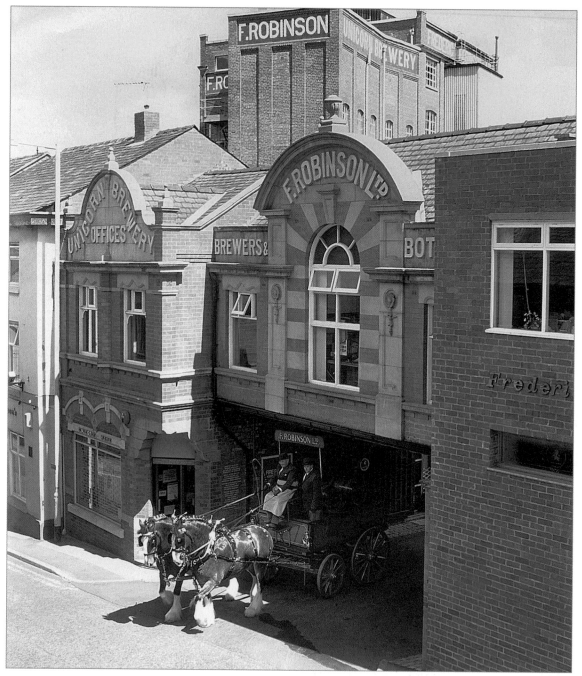

Frederick Robinson Ltd's Unicorn Brewery, 1980s. The Robinson enterprise thrived and when Frederick died in 1890 the *Stockport Advertiser* wrote in his obituary that 'very recently important alterations have been carried out at the brewery, the structure having been considerably enlarged, the brewing plant thoroughly modernised, and the fittings of a first class brewery having been put in so as to enable the firm to cope with their large and increasing trade'. Between 1925 and 1929 Robinson's constructed a new brewhouse and its ornate seven-storey tower, complete with unicorns in the stonework, remains a distinctive feature of the Stockport landscape today.

The Felinfoel brewhouse decorated for the coronation of King George VI, May 1937. Felinfoel is the oldest brewery still operating in Wales and continues to be a family-owned business. The present brewery buildings date from 1870 and have Grade II listed status. Felinfoel is a small village adjacent to Llanelli. The brewery was founded by David John, whose family had local tinplate, iron and mining interests. During the mid-1830s he purchased the King's Head Hotel in Felinfoel and later renamed it the Union Inn. Beer was brewed for consumption on the premises and later for sale further afield.

Felinfoel Brewery decorated for the coronation of Queen Elizabeth II, 1953. The depression in South Wales during the 1930s was so severe that free bread and cheese were given away with pints of beer purchased in Felinfoel pubs. Despite the success of its bold canning venture (see p. 94), Felinfoel Brewery struggled financially in the decades after the Second World War. During the 1970s, however, with financial fortunes improving, Felinfoel's old wooden fermenting vessels were replaced by stainless steel versions and a new copper vat replaced the original open, coal-fired one, which had been patched up over the years to keep it working.

The earliest design of beer can from Felinfoel Brewery, 1935. Felinfoel's greatest claim to fame is as the first European brewery to can beer (see p. 44). On 3 December 1935 the *Llanelli & County Guardian* recorded the event with the headlines 'Canned Beer Arrives', 'Epoch-making Process at Felinfoel Brewery', and 'New Hope for Tinplate Industry'. Conical 10oz cans were filled on an adapted bottling machine and the first can went on public sale on 19 March 1936.

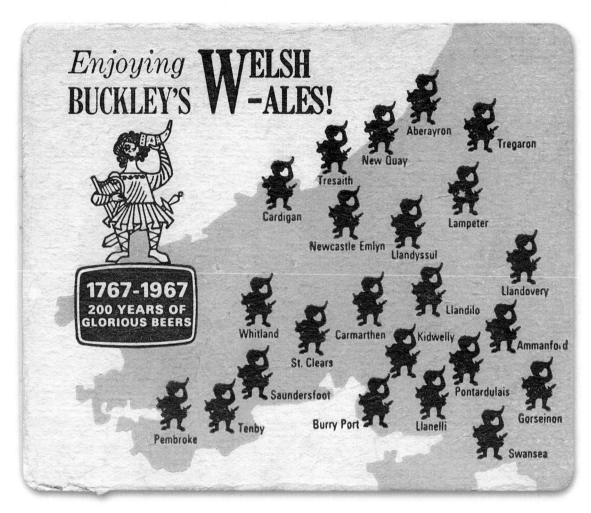

A promotional beer mat from 1967 illustrating the area of South Wales in which beers from Buckley's Brewery Ltd were available. For many years Felinfoel operated in the shadow of Buckley's, so it is ironic that while Felinfoel is a thriving business today, Buckley's is no more. In 1997 S.A. Brain & Company Ltd purchased Crown Buckley, the second principal independent brewer in South Wales, formed by the merger of Buckley's and the Crown Brewery of Pontyclun. Buckley's Llanelli brewery – where brewing had taken place since 1779 – was closed the following year.

Opposite: The Buckley Bros' Brewery, Llanelli, 1880s. Buckley's Brewery was Felinfoel's chief rival, and as the company had also been keen to develop canned beers, its owners were less than pleased when Felinfoel was able to market a successful canned beer first. In 1965 Buckley's mounted an abortive takeover attempt after members of the John family put their Felinfoel shares on the market.

Brain's 'Old Brewery', Cardiff, 1880s. The independent Welsh brewing firm of S.A. Brain & Company was established at the Old Brewery in Cardiff in 1882 by Samuel Arthur Brain and his uncle Joseph Benjamin Brain. Brewing had been taking place on the Old Brewery site since 1713. In 1999 the Cardiff Brewery (formerly Hancock's), in which the Brain's and Buckley's ranges of ales are now produced, was acquired from Bass.

S.A. Brain & Company's 'New Brewery', Cardiff, with the Old Brewery on the left. The New Brewery was established in 1887, and shortly afterwards, when visiting Cardiff to research his *Noted Breweries of Great Britain & Ireland*, Alfred Barnard wrote that 'more than a hundred years have gone by since the Cardiff Old Brewery was built, and when the visitor contrasts its old grey walls and confined proportions with the brand-new brewery that overshadows it, he is amazed to see from what small beginnings the business (which has now reached such vast proportions) has sprung.'

The North & Scotland

Scottish Courage Ltd is a major player on the north of England brewing scene: Britain's largest brewing group operates the John Smith Brewery at Tadcaster in North Yorkshire and the Tyne Brewery in Newcastle upon Tyne. North of the border, Scottish Courage runs Edinburgh's Fountain Brewery, and dominates the volume market along with Interbrew, courtesy of its Tennent's Wellpark Brewery in Glasgow. Important northern regional brewers include Jennings Brothers plc in Cumbria and Camerons Brewery Ltd in Hartlepool, Cleveland, along with the Northern Clubs' Federation Brewery Ltd on Tyneside. In Scotland the Belhaven Group plc of Dunbar in East Lothian keeps the flag flying for the larger independents. Yorkshire leads the way in terms of micro-brewers, with around fifty currently active, while Scotland has also seen heartening growth in the development of imaginative, small-scale brewing ventures in recent years.

Head brewer Ian Cameron tests the temperature of the wort after it has passed through the Traquair House Brewery wort cooler, 1990s.

Tadcaster, North Yorkshire, *c.* 1912, featuring John Smith's Brewery. It is recorded that there were brewhouses in Tadcaster in 1341, and like Burton upon Trent and Edinburgh, Tadcaster developed into a brewing centre because of the quality of its water. Soft water was usually considered ideal for brewing. Here it was hard, but it was rich in sulphate from the underlying Magnesian limestone and that was significant in the production of good beer. Three breweries survive in the town today, namely John Smith's Brewery, the small independent Old Brewery of Samuel Smith, and Coors' Tower Brewery on Wetherby Road.

John Smith's Brewery, Tadcaster, late 1960s. The brewery was constructed in 1879, and when Alfred Barnard visited Tadcaster during the late 1880s, he wrote that 'this brewery stands entitled, not only to as high a place as any other in Yorkshire, but also, and more especially on account of its marvellous progress, on an equality with those of Burton and Edinburgh. It is the centre of industry in the town, and within its walls as many as 200 persons are employed.' Today the brewery is owned by Scottish & Newcastle plc.

Joshua Tetley & Son's Brewery, Leeds, from Crown Point Maltings, early 1920s. Crown Point Maltings were built in 1866, and served the brewery until their closure in 1972. Brewing has taken place on the site of the present Tetley Brewery in Leeds since 1792, and under the Tetley name since 1822. In that year, Joshua Tetley – from a family of Yorkshire maltsters – took over the brewery established by William Sykes, paying £400 for it. In 1866 the brewery was rebuilt on a substantially larger scale than the original, and by 1874 the company was selling over 160,000 barrels of beer per year.

The cask-washing shed, Tetley's Brewery, Leeds, early 1920s. After visiting Tetley's Brewery during the late 1880s, Alfred Barnard noted that 'as many as 2,418 casks have been passed through the washing sheds in one day. An entry of 2,000 casks is a frequent occurrence.' The company employed 400 brewery workers at the time of Barnard's visit. Today the brewery is operated by Carlsberg-Tetley Brewing Ltd, and is the largest dedicated cask ale brewery in Britain. It is located on a site that covers 20 acres and includes a new brewhouse built in 1989 – situated just yards from where the original one stood.

A Theakston staff group, probably 1920s. Robert Theakston leased the Black Bull Inn and brewhouse in Masham from 1827, and in 1875 his son Thomas built the present brewery. The rival Lightfoot's Brewery was bought in 1919, principally, it is claimed, to acquire its fine cricket team! Theakston was taken over by Matthew Brown & Co Ltd of Blackburn in 1984, which three years later was acquired in turn by Scottish & Newcastle Ltd. In 2003 the Theakston brewery and brands were sold back to members of the Theakston family, headed by Simon Theakston, great-great-grandson of the founder.

York Brewery Company Ltd's managing director Tony Thomson shows a group of visitors around the brewery, late 1990s. When the micro-brewery on Toft Green opened in 1996, commercial brewing was restored to the historic city for the first time in forty years. York has a twenty-barrel brew-plant with a purpose-built viewing gallery. The small-scale copper and open mash tun can be seen here. More than 400 pubs are served, and the brewery also owns three outlets in York (see p. 139).

Castle Eden Brewery, County Durham, shortly after its closure in 2002. In 1826 John Nimmo took over the Castle Inn in Castle Eden, and by 1844 he was also brewing there. The brewery of J. Nimmo & Son Ltd retained its independence until 1963, when it was acquired by Whitbread & Co Ltd. A management buy-out took place in 1998, but following the purchase of Camerons Brewery Ltd in 2002 it was decided to concentrate brewing at Cameron's Lion Brewery in nearby Hartlepool, and Castle Eden brewery was closed. Most of the site was cleared for residential development.

Cameron's Lion Brewery, Hartlepool, 2002. Brewing was begun on the present site by William Waldon in 1852 and the business was later taken over by John William Cameron. Most of the brewery structure visible in this photograph dates from a major rebuild in 1892. The site was in the hands of Wolverhampton & Dudley Breweries plc at the time of its acquisition by Castle Eden for £35 million. Today the Lion Brewery produces a range of ales which includes the popular Strongarm Bitter, first launched in 1955. It also brews the principal Castle Eden brands – Nimmo's XXXX and Castle Eden Ale.

THE TYNE BREWERY, NEWCASTLE UPON TYNE
Home of Newcastle Blue Star Beers

The Tyne Brewery, Newcastle upon Tyne, 1970s. Newcastle Breweries was founded in 1890 by the amalgamation of five local companies, including Barras & Co. Barras owned the Tyne Brewery, which was to form the heart of the new operation and was a high-capacity plant built in the late 1860s. Newcastle Breweries Ltd merged in 1960 with Scottish Brewers Ltd, becoming Scottish & Newcastle Breweries. By 1970 the brewery was turning out three million barrels per annum and had been greatly upgraded. Today, the brewery produces a wide selection of brands, including the famous Newcastle Brown Ale and Exhibition Ale.

A cask-cleaning machine in the Northern Clubs' Federation Brewery, Hanover Square, Newcastle upon Tyne, probably 1950s. The 'Fed' was set up in 1919 by a group of north-eastern working men's club members who were frustrated at the lack of available beer during the thirsty years following the First World War. From 1927 until 1980 the Federation operated from this brewery in Hanover Square, and by the outbreak of the Second World War expansion and modernisation had raised its capacity to 2,300 barrels and 10,000 bottles per week. Further expansion in 1957 increased output to 7,500 barrels and 50,000 bottles per week (see p. 46).

The Workington Brewery, *c.* 1925. The brewery
was located in Ladies' Walk, Workington,
Cumbria, and dated from 1792. It was owned by
the Iredale family. In 1975 it was acquired by
Matthew Brown & Co Ltd, which closed the
Workington Brewery in 1986, two years after
taking over the T&R Theakston operation. For a
time Workington was used by Matthew Brown to
brew Theakston's beers because the Masham
brewery was already working to full capacity.
In its heyday the Workington Brewery was a
major rival to Jennings' Brothers of
Cockermouth (see p. 104).

Below: Loading a dray for delivery at John Booth's
Old Brewery in Ulverston, Lancashire, probably
1880s. The Old Brewery dated from 1755, and in
1896 it was bought by the Hartley brothers,
Robert and Peter, of Burnley. In 1982 Stockport-
based Frederick Robinson Ltd took over Hartley's
Brewery, subsequently closing it in 1991. The
Hartley's name is perpetuated, however, in
Hartley's XB and the recently introduced Hartley's
Cumbria Way.

Jennings Brothers' Castle Brewery, Cockermouth, probably pre-First World War. John Jennings senior started brewing beer in the village of Lorton, between Keswick and Cockermouth, in 1828. At that time Cumberland boasted twenty-eight breweries. In 1874 Jennings moved to their present home in Cockermouth, where the Castle Brewery stands next to Cockermouth Castle and close to the confluence of the Cocker and Derwent rivers. Jennings Brothers plc is now the only remaining significant independent brewery in Cumbria and major expansion and upgrading work was undertaken to increase brewery capacity between 1999 and 2002.

A selection of Jennings' bottled beers of various vintages. Today Jennings is best known for its cask ales, including Cumberland Ale, Sneck Lifter and Cocker Hoop, which are also available in bottled form. Jennings uses malt from Norfolk-grown Maris Otter barley, Fuggles hops from Herefordshire and Goldings hops from Kent, along with pure Lake District water from its own well, to create its highly regarded range of ales.

A Belhaven beer label from the 1950s, featuring the popular character 'Belhaven Bill'. For 250 years Belhaven brewery was a family-owned venture, trading as Dudgeon & Co from 1815. In 1972, however, the company was sold to a pub and hotel chain, and passed through various hands before a management buy-out took place in 1993. Belhaven is one of the very few independent Scottish breweries to survive through the 1960s. Today it produces cask and keg ales, and brews and bottles under contract for a wide range of other brewers. Belhaven Best is now the leading keg beer brand in Scotland.

George Howell, head brewer at Belhaven Brewery, Dunbar, 2001. Brewing has taken place in the coastal town of Dunbar, some 30 miles from Edinburgh, since Benedictine monks sunk wells and dug storage vaults at Belhaven some time before the sixteenth century. Remarkably, two Benedictine wells and the vaults survive, and are incorporated into the present structures. Belhaven is the oldest working brewery in Scotland, and the Belhaven Group plc is the largest regional brewer north of the border.

The former Lochside Brewery, Montrose, Angus, 1990s. Lochside was owned by James Deuchar Ltd, and was built during the 1890s in uncompromising German brauhaus style on the site of an eighteenth-century brewery. The business of James Deuchar Ltd was acquired by Newcastle Breweries Ltd in 1956 and the brewery was closed, subsequently being converted into a distillery which operated until 1992. The future of the arresting structure is in doubt at the time of writing.

Traquair House Brewery's head brewer Ian Cameron draws a sample from a fermenting vessel, 1990s. Traquair House Brewery Ltd is situated alongside the Maxwell-Stuart family's magnificent Traquair House at Innerleithen in the Scottish Borders. A brewery was operating at Traquair when Mary Queen of Scots visited the house in 1566, and the nucleus of the present building dates from the eighteenth century. In 1965 the disused brewery was discovered by Peter Maxwell-Stuart, who proceeded to return it to working order. Despite modest expansion, all ale is still fermented in the 200-year-old oak vessels pictured.

Staff at John Wright & Co's North Methven Street Brewery, Perth, undated. The worker on the left is drinking bottled beer from a tin mug, and the barrel appears to have been hastily prepared for the photograph. A brewery was in existence in North Methven Street by 1786, and by 1900 Wright's was not only brewing its own range of ales, but also bottling Guinness and Burton Ales under licence. Wright & Co survived until 1961 when the company was acquired by Sunderland-based Vaux Breweries Ltd, who closed it soon after purchase. The site is now occupied by a housing development.

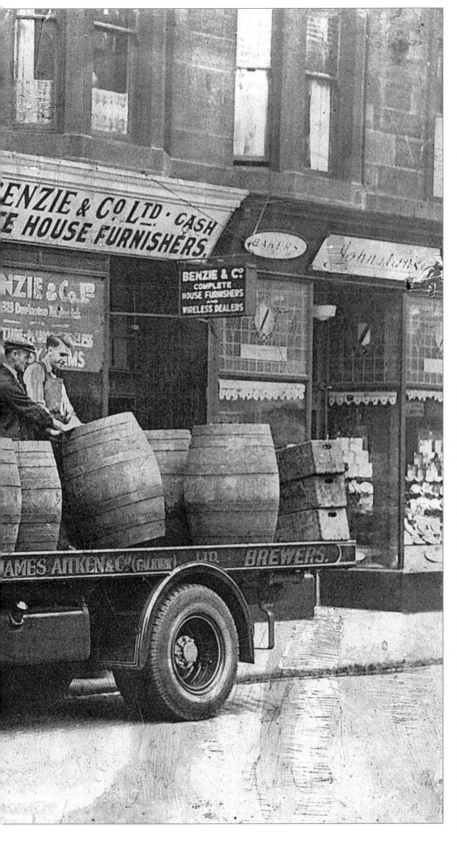

Delivering ale from the Falkirk brewery of James Aitken & Co to the Criterion Bar on Dumbarton Road, Glasgow, probably late 1940s. When Alfred Barnard visited Aitken's during the 1880s, it was one of Scotland's leading 'regional' brewers with a notable export trade. Barnard wrote, 'It is not surprising that a product so excellent as Aitken's beer and so wholesome and refreshing, should have become the standard drink in Australia and the colonies.' Aitken's had been founded in 1740 and remained in family ownership for more than two centuries, finally closing in the mid-1960s after its acquisition by Northern Breweries.

William Younger & Co Ltd's Holyrood and Abbey breweries, Edinburgh, 1950s, with the Palace of Holyroodhouse on the right. The Holyrood Brewery is located to the left of the Abbey Brewery in the photograph. The Holyrood Brewery site is now home to a residential development, and during the 1990s the Abbey Brewery buildings were demolished to make way for the new Scottish Parliament.

Opposite, top: Abbey Brewery bottling hall, early 1950s. William Younger reputedly started work in 1749 at the age of sixteen in Anderson's Leith brewery, but died when he was just thirty-seven. In 1777 one of his sons, Archibald, set up a brewery in the grounds of the abbey of Holyroodhouse, and by the early 1820s various family brewing concerns had been unified under the banner of William Younger & Co. The Abbey Brewery had opened during the 1820s, but by the mid-1950s it was only being used on a seasonal basis, and was subsequently converted into company offices.

Opposite, bottom: Holyrood Brewery coppers, early 1950s. The Holyrood Brewery was established in 1864, and such was the scale of business conducted there and at Abbey that in 1886 Younger & Co brewed some 215,000 barrels of beer, which was around one-sixth of the total produced in the whole of Scotland. In 1931 William Younger & Co Ltd and William McEwan & Co Ltd combined to form Scottish Brewers Ltd, which in turn became part of Scottish & Newcastle Breweries in 1960. In 1986 the Holyrood Brewery closed, bringing to an end a very long tradition of brewing in the Canongate area of the city.

Inspection of William McEwan & Co Ltd's draymen and horses, Fountain Brewery, 29 April 1929. McEwan expanded his brewery over the years, and when his firm became a limited company in 1889 it had capital of £1 million. When he died William McEwan left personal assets of more than £1.5 million, despite having been a noted philanthropist, gifting the McEwan Hall to Edinburgh University and purchasing a Rembrandt for the National Gallery. In 1973 Scottish & Newcastle Breweries Ltd spent £13 million constructing a new Fountain Brewery and this is now the company's sole Scottish plant.

William McEwan (1827–1913). William McEwan was born in Alloa in 1827, the son of a ship owner, and his sister married into the Younger brewing family of Candleriggs Brewery in Alloa. William joined the Heriot Brewery in Edinburgh's Grassmarket in 1851, and five years later, backed by his in-laws and with borrowed money, he set up his own Fountain Brewery in the Fountainbridge district of the city. McEwan began to export his beers from the 1860s, taking advantage of his family's maritime connections in the process. Australia, New Zealand, the West Indies and India were principal markets for McEwan's Export and India Pale Ale.

Maclay's Thistle brewery, Alloa, shortly after its closure in August 1999. Alloa once boasted eight breweries, and the Maclay Group plc has its origins in a brewing operation established at Alloa's Mills Brewery in 1830 by James Maclay. The brewery pictured dates from 1870, but by the late 1990s required substantial investment to give it a viable future. Instead, Maclay chose to have its range of beers produced on a contract basis, and at the time of writing the brewery faces demolition to make way for redevelopment of the town centre site.

An 1884 bottling hall at the former Younger's Export bottling department, Kelliebank, Alloa, now home to the Forth Brewery Co Ltd. Most of the bottling complex was burnt down in 1961, but this building survived and continues to have a role in Alloa's brewing heritage. George Younger & Son Ltd built its bottling plant at Kelliebank, beside the River Forth, as demand for bottled beers for export grew dramatically during the 1880s. The first carbonating and chilling plant in Scotland was installed at Kelliebank in 1903. The Forth is now the only operational brewery in Alloa.

The staff of George Younger & Son, *c.* 1890, at Candleriggs Brewery, Alloa, with barrels of Revolver brand ale and a framed showcard featuring India Pale Ale. George Younger set up what was almost certainly the first commercial brewery in Alloa in 1762, and by 1890 it was brewing up to 25,000 barrels of ale per year. Younger's was the third largest Scottish brewing company after the Edinburgh pair of William McEwan and William Younger. In 1960 the family-run company was taken over by United Breweries, which in turn merged with the Charrington organisation two years later, and in 1963 Candleriggs Brewery closed.

The Grange Brewery, Alloa, c. 1920. The Grange had begun life around 1795 as a whisky distillery, but was converted to a brewery in about 1837. It subsequently traded as the Bass Crest Brewery, and use of this name led to legal action on behalf of the Burton upon Trent brewing giant on a number of occasions. The brewery was purchased in 1919 by George Younger & Son Ltd, and was subsequently used for the production of non-alcoholic beer and stout in order to safeguard Younger's business in the event of the Temperance Party achieving major success.

The brewhouse, Alloa Brewery, c. 1990. The original Alloa Brewery opened in 1810 and was purchased in 1866 by Archibald Arrol. The business traded as Archibald Arrol & Sons Ltd until 1951, when it was taken over by Ind Coope. The brewery began to brew lager in 1921, creating Graham's Golden Lager, later re-branded as Skol. In addition to Skol, the Alloa Brewery produced such perennial Scottish keg favourites as Alloa's Diamond Heavy and Alloa's Export until its closure in 1998 as part of a Carlsberg-Tetley rationalisation programme. This occurred despite recent investment of around £2.5 million in the Whins Road plant.

Women workers cleaning large storage vats at Tennent's Wellpark Brewery during the First World War. It is recorded that in 1556 Robert Tennent was a private brewer and maltman based near Glasgow Cathedral, and in 1776 Tennent's set up in business as public brewers and maltsters in the Drygate area, now incorporated into the company's present Wellpark complex. In 1793 it took over the neighbouring Wellpark Brewery, and by the middle of the nineteenth century, Tennent's was the largest exporter of ale in Britain.

Three generations of delivery vehicles, embracing horse power, steam power (extreme right) and petrol power on display at Tennent's Wellpark Brewery, *c.* 1930. By the early 1880s Henniger Lager was on sale in select licensed grocers in Glasgow and faced with the growing availability of continental lagers, it seemed logical for Tennent's to begin its own lager brewing venture. A German lager brewer by the name of Jacob Klinger and a Dane called Eric Westergaard were employed to oversee the development of lager brewing at Wellpark. Tennent's became the first brewers in Britain to produce lager when the new venture came on stream in May 1885.

A woman filling a cask at Wellpark Brewery during the First World War. Despite the scepticism of the Glasgow press, which dubbed Tennent's pioneering lager brewery a 'madman's dream', lager production enabled the company to survive through the difficult trading times of the early twentieth century. A hundred years previously, Glasgow had boasted more than twenty breweries, and there were still fourteen in the city in 1900. However, only J. & R. Tennent Ltd survived beyond the Second World War. The company lost its independence in 1963, and today Wellpark is one of five British breweries operated by Interbrew.

5

Drinking Beer

The Rose Street brew-pub, Edinburgh, 1980s. Scotland's first 'brew-pub', the Rose Street Brewery, was owned by the Alloa Brewery Company, and opened in 1983 in the former White Cockade pub. The brewery closed in 2000, following the cessation of brewing in Alloa by the Alloa Brewery Company's parent Carlsberg-Tetley. Today the pub, situated on one of Edinburgh's principal drinking thoroughfares, continues to be a popular haunt of locals and tourists alike.

As we have seen, monks were some of the first innkeepers, offering accommodation to travellers and quenching their thirsts with home-brewed ale. According to Frederick Hackwood in *Inns, Ales and Drinking Customs of Old England*, 'certain it is that inns made their appearance in this country with the very earliest dawn of civilisation'. He notes that when the Romans arrived in Britain after 43 AD and began their famous programme of road-building, they sited alongside them 'houses of entertainment for man and horse, which were the Roman equivalent for, and prototype of, the good old English wayside hostelry'. He observes that by the seventh century there were ale-houses in Britain, and the 'Laws' of King Ethelbert of Kent (616) contain regulations regarding 'eala-hus'. In 1577, a census recorded the existence of 19,759 inns, taverns and alehouses in England and Wales. With a total population of 3.7 million, that equated to a remarkable figure of one place of 'refreshment' for every 187 people.

Hackwood notes that an Act passed during 1603, the first year of the reign of King James I, defined 'the antient, true, and principal use of inns, ale-houses, and victualling houses' to be for the 'resort, relief, and lodging of wayfaring people, travelling from place to place, and for such supply of the wants of such people as are not able by greater quantities to make provision of victual'. The preamble then proceeds to lay down that such inns 'are not meant for entertainment and harbouring of lewd idle people, to spend and consume their time and their money in lewd and drunken manner'.

In more modern times, the most significant piece of legislation affecting public houses was the Beer Act of 1830. With the passing of this Act, designed in part to curb excessive consumption of gin, any rate-payer could obtain an excise licence to sell beer from his home on payment of two guineas. By the end of the year no fewer than 24,000 new 'beerhouses' had been opened in England and Wales, and four years later a further 22,000 had been established. Not everyone approved of the new Act. The essayist and *bon viveur* the Revd Sydney Smith lamented that 'everyone is drunk. Those who are not singing are sprawling. The sovereign people are in a beastly state.'

By the later 1870s many brewers had begun to purchase their own retail outlets rather than sell beer to independent licensees. This notion of 'tied houses' developed as fierce competition raged between rival brewers. One of its principal attractions was that it gave brewers a clear idea of how much beer to brew. Owning outlets gave them guaranteed sales, and in addition to purchasing existing public houses, brewers also embarked on programmes of construction, with new hostelries often being designed along rather grand and sumptuous lines. Between 1886 and 1900 no fewer than 234 breweries went public in order to raise funds, principally to enable them to acquire or build public houses. At the time, beer-drinking was in a period of comparative decline, partly due to a growth of interest in sports such as cricket and football among working men, along with the activities of the Temperance Movement, and an end to 'free-licensing' in 1869, when magistrates were granted the responsibility of issuing licences.

A number of major brewing companies tried to ignore the 'tied house' concept. Among their number were the Yorkshire firm of Joshua Tetley & Son and Samuel Allsopp & Co of Burton upon Trent. Tetley saw rivals buy up all the prime outlets to which it had once sold beer and was finally forced to enter the acquisitions market, while Allsopp was convinced, wrongly as it turned out, that the quality of the company's ales, marketed as 'the best beers in the world', would alone ensure continuing prosperity. Sales fell from 824,600 barrels in 1884 to 540,000 seven years later and in the decade from 1892 Allsopp rapidly acquired 1,200 public houses to restore its position, but the cost of doing so was ruinous.

During the twentieth century British public houses changed remarkably little until after the Second World War. Then, during the 1960s and '70s, brewers realised that they had to do more to get people into their pubs, and, in particular, attract uncommitted drinkers. Food, entertainment and overall ambience tended to become more important than the variety and quality of beer on offer, with bland keg beers and lagers very much in the ascendancy. In the early 1970s, lager represented just 3 per cent of British total beer sales, whereas in 2004 it accounted for more than half all beer sales.

Many new pubs were built during the 1960s and '70s, and old ones were often brutally made over. During the last three decades, the Campaign for Real Ale has lobbied not only on behalf of traditional cask ales, but also to preserve the most interesting and historical architectural features in public houses. In recent years, however, the very existence of many pubs has been threatened, particularly in rural areas, as social habits have changed, despite the introduction of more liberal licensing laws, allowing for the option of all-day opening. According to CAMRA, in late 2003 twenty pubs closed each month in Britain.

A significant development of the last two decades has been the retreat of many larger brewing companies from 'vertically integrated' operations in which breweries serve a core market of managed or tenanted public houses. Great names such as Bass and Whitbread, as well as a host of regional brewers such as Greenall Whitley & Co Ltd in the North-West of England, have abandoned brewing entirely in order to operate estates of pubs and other leisure enterprises. Their beers and lagers are now brewed for them under contract by third parties, thus destroying the historic links between brands and locality. This has led to the rise of what are often termed 'pubcos', which have now replaced brewers as the largest retailers of beer in Britain. Industry leaders Punch Taverns and Enterprise Inns now control some 15,000 pubs, compared to 10,000 owned by brewing companies.

Thanks largely to the efforts of CAMRA, the keg and lager revolution in British pubs has been offset to a modest degree by a growth of interest in 'real' ales, and more pubs are now offering drinkers a choice of regional or local cask beers, alongside the ubiquitous national and international keg brands.

An early morning delivery at Cheshire brewer Frederick Robinson's Waggon & Horses public house, at Matley, between Mottram and Stalybridge, *c*. 1890. The premises were built as a farmhouse in 1663 and became a coaching inn in 1789. It was originally known as the Sawmill Inn and was bought by Robinson's in 1910.

Above: Charlie, the last of Shepherd Neame's dray horses, delivering beer to the Castle Inn, Ashford, Kent, during the 1960s. When Charlie died the brewery's stabling was used to expand the bottling store and warehouse.

Delivering a cask of Everard's ale to a pub cellar, 1950s. The draymen's job involved a great deal of physical labour, and thirsts were quenched in pre-breathalyser days by copious pints of the product at pubs along the way.

Customers relishing their pints of Shepherd Neame ale, Kent, 1940s.

The beer cellar at Ye Olde Trip to Jerusalem, Nottingham, undated. This inn stands at the foot of the castle rock in Nottingham, and its interior walls are carved out of the sandstone beneath the castle. Brewing took place in the cave cellars under the inn until some forty years ago, and the cellar remains much the same today as it did when this photograph was taken, except that the wooden casks have been replaced by aluminium kegs.

A licensed house cellar, featuring casks of Whitbread ale, 1950s. The most significant change between methods of serving beer in the 1950s and today is that half a century ago all beer was delivered from wooden casks by handpump, whereas today most beer is transported in aluminium kegs and is raised from cellars by gas pressure. Pasteurised, sterile keg beer is attractive to the publican as it keeps for longer than cask beer without deteriorating, and requires less attention in order to produce consistent pints. Critics, however, complain that keg beers lack the character of cask ales.

Ye Olde Trip to Jerusalem, Nottingham, undated. It is often claimed that this inn is the oldest in England, and though it is impossible to substantiate the foundation date of 1189AD, it is known that Nottingham Castle certainly had a working brewhouse in the immediate vicinity prior to that date. In 1189 Richard I became king and mounted a crusade to fight the Saracens in the Holy Land. People planning to join the crusade would gather at royal strongholds such as Nottingham Castle, and in Middle English a 'trip' was a resting place where journeys were broken, hence the inn's name.

The Seven Stars, Withy Grove, Manchester, c. 1900. At the time of this photograph, the Seven Stars also claimed to be the oldest public house in Britain. The area of Manchester in which it was located was heavily redeveloped during the twentieth century, most notably in the 1970s, and no trace of the Seven Stars remains. Close to its site stands Manchester's oldest pub, the Old Wellington Inn, which probably dates from the mid-fifteenth century. It survived the 1996 IRA bombing of Manchester, despite significant damage, and remains the last timber box-framed building in the city.

The First and Last Inn, Sennen, Cornwall, probably 1950s. This popular inn close to Land's End dates from 1620, and is one of the county's oldest and most original drinking places. A viewing panel in the floor allows a glimpse of the ancient tunnels beneath the pub, perhaps used by smugglers in former times. According to *Slater's Trade Directory* of 1852, 'here [at Sennen] is an inn with a remarkable sign being "the first and last Inn in England".'

The Radjel Inn, Pendeen, Cornwall, 1973. Until 1973 this was the Boscaswell Inn, but in that year it was renamed by the St Austell Brewery Co Ltd in honour of its much-loved landlord, seventy-two-year old Willie Warren. Warren's great-great-grandfather had been nicknamed Radjel, a Cornish term for a pile of stones where a fox makes its home, and his family ran the pub for a total of ninety-nine years. Willie Warren died in 1980, aged seventy-nine, and still holds the record for the longest-serving St Austell Brewery landlord, having held the licence for fifty-nine years.

The Leather Bottle, Cobham, Surrey, 1904. This inn featured in Charles Dickens's *Pickwick Papers*, and, according to the signage, offered 'Meux & Co's celebrated London Porter and Double Stout'. At the time the photograph was taken, porter was still a popular drink in the London area, and Meux's Brewery Co Ltd was based at the Horseshoe Brewery in the Tottenham Court Road.

Ye Old Fighting Cocks, St Albans, probably 1950s, advertising Benskin's ales and stout, brewed in Watford. Ye Old Fighting Cocks dates from the eleventh century, and the distinctive, octagonal building was originally a timber-framed pigeon house close to St Albans Abbey. After the dissolution of the abbey in 1539, the structure was taken down and rebuilt in its present location on the banks of the River Ver. Ye Old Fighting Cocks tends to vie with Ye Olde Trip to Jerusalem in Nottingham (see p. 131) for the accolade of being the oldest surviving pub in England.

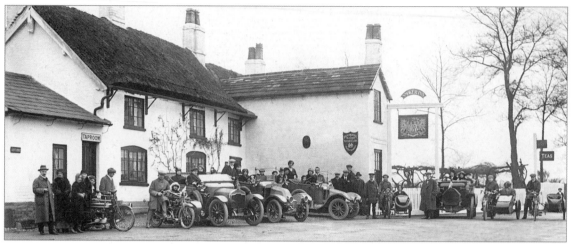

The Smoker Inn, a Frederick Robinson house at Plumley, near Knutsford, Cheshire, *c.* 1910. The local motor rally is about to set off on an outing in a wide assortment of vehicles. Frederick Robinson bought his first pub in 1876 to act as a showcase for his beers and to guarantee that they were served in the optimum condition – often a frustrating problem for responsible brewers who lost control of the product once it left their breweries. By 1910 the estate comprised in excess of thirty houses, a figure which has now risen to around the 400 mark.

King William IV public house in Earl Shilton, Leicestershire, probably pre-First World War. The King William IV was one of the first pubs to be acquired by William Everard, trading from 1869, and is still part of the estate of Everards Brewery Ltd today.

M.H. Choppin's Cambria Stores, Camberwell, London, with Mr and Mrs Choppin in the doorway, *c*. 1900. The window and delivery cart advertise Thorne's Grey Horse Brand Beers, brewed by Thorne Brothers Ltd of Nine Elms Brewery in South London. The Thorne family acquired the brewery in 1841 and it was sold to Meux's Brewery Co Ltd in 1914. It then operated for a further fifty years.

Regulars gather outside the Bull's Head Inn, Ashford-in-the-Water in Derbyshire's Peak District, at the start of the local penny farthing rally, 1885.

The Alvanley Arms at Cotebrook near Tarporley in Cheshire, 1920s. As this picture shows, a drive to a country pub is a longer-established tradition than we might realise, and in those pre-war days, four decades prior to the introduction of the breathalyser test for motorists, drinking and driving mixed without any social stigma.

The Elephant & Castle Tavern, London, 1890s. According to *The Licensed Victuallers' Year Book* for 1900, 'for generations the Elephant and Castle Tavern has been known throughout the English-speaking population of the world'. It was established during the reign of Queen Elizabeth I, and the structure in the photograph was built in 1816, being demolished in 1898 to make way for a new, enlarged Elephant & Castle Hotel. The tavern was owned by Truman, Hanbury, Buxton & Co Ltd of the Black Eagle Brewery in Stepney, one of the largest British brewers at the time.

The Ship Inn, Little Thurrock, Grays, Essex, early twentieth century. The inn offered 'Fine Ales, Stout and Porter' from the local Hornchurch Brewery. The man in the doorway wearing a waistcoat and white shirt is believed to be the landlord, R. Whitby.

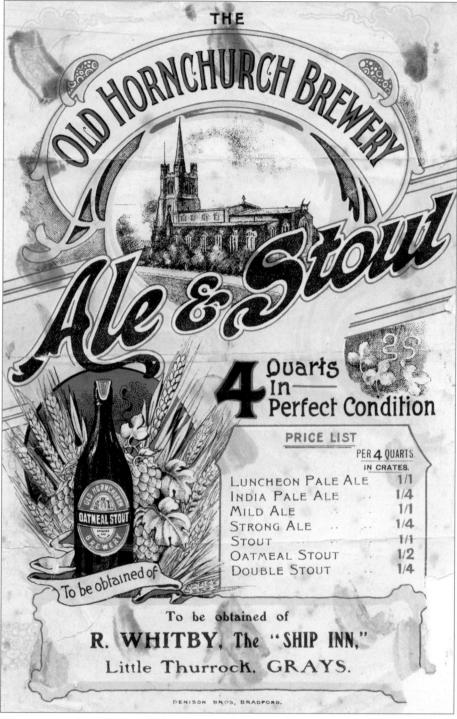

An advert for the Old Hornchurch Brewery, featuring the Ship Inn (see previous page). The brewery was founded in 1789, and in his *Handbook to the Environs of London* (1876), James Thorne wrote of Hornchurch that 'it has a good-sized brewery (Woodfine's)'. By 1905 the brewery was in the hands of S.R. Conron, formerly of the Francis Court Brewery in Dublin, and in 1924 the company was bought by Harman's Uxbridge Brewery, which was sold to Mann's the following year. Brewing ceased in 1929.

The York Brewery's Last Drop Inn on Colliergate, in York's city centre, *c.* 2000. This was the first of three pubs to be acquired by the York Brewery Co Ltd (see p. 100), and was opened in 2000. It is based in a former solicitor's office, and thrives by offering York Brewery ales, good food, live music and a ban on what *The Good Beer Guide* calls 'electronic amusements'.

Painter's shop, Hardys and Hansons Kimberley Brewery, Nottingham, 1982. Pictorial inn signs developed when literacy levels were very low, and indicated a place to drink. The earliest British inns tended to have religious names, such as the Cross Keys (the emblem of St Peter), the Star (of Bethlehem), or the Bull (a Papal dictat). Once Henry VIII started the Reformation in the sixteenth century, many publicans decided discretion was the better part of valour, and began to give their pubs irreproachably loyal names like the King's Head, the Crown, the Rising Sun and the Rose, the latter two being symbols of Henry and his Tudor dynasty.

The wrong way and the right way to serve a public house customer, as demonstrated in a trade manual of the 1950s. In the second photograph, the barman wears a jacket to cover his braces, and the cigarette is gone from his mouth. Better still, his fingers no longer appear to be in the customer's beer! The dirty rag over the beer pump has disappeared, and the 'empties' have been cleared away. A plate of well-cut sandwiches has appeared in their place.

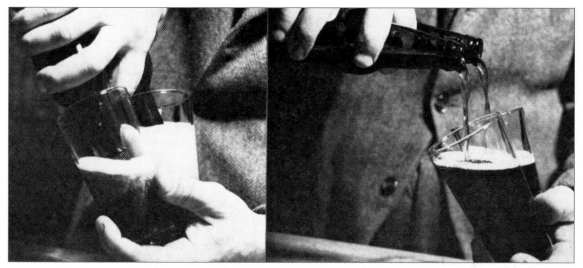

Bottle pouring – the wrong way and the right way. In the second picture, the glasses have been angled so that the beer flows into them without creating an excess head, and the pourer's fingers are more hygienically positioned.

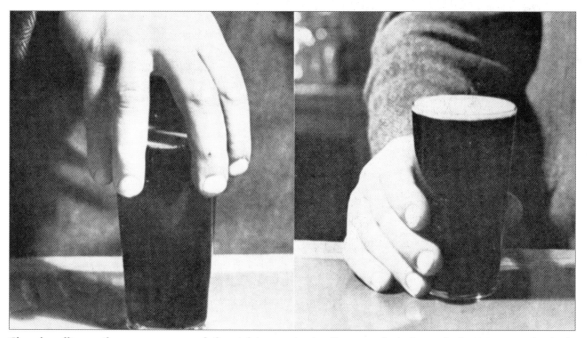

Glass handling – the wrong way and the right way. Again, the second photograph shows a more hygienic way of presenting the glass of beer.

ACKNOWLEDGEMENTS

Many people have taken time and trouble to provide photographs and information for this book, and I am most grateful to them all. Thanks are due to John Alden, Miranda Askew, Norman Barber, Frances Brace, Rob Bruce, Dave Cartwright, Eric Fower, Brian Glover, R.W.D. Hanson, Michael Hardman, Ian Hulland, Miles Jenner, Mac Joseph, Julie Knight, Philip Lewis, Catherine Lister, June Mitchell, Jenny Panter, John Preston, Weibke Redlich, Nelion Ridley, Dennis Robinson, George Newman, Berry Ritchie, Anna Skelton, David Smith, Donald Smith, Ruth Smith, Catherine Maxwell Stuart, Sasha Taylor, Tony Thomson, Alma Topen, Colin Valentine and Steve Wilson. Last, but far from least, the staff of Sutton Publishing, and in particular Sarah Bryce and Michelle Tilling, deserve my thanks for their unfailing helpfulness and good humour.

Photographs are reproduced by kind permission of the following:
Everards Brewery Ltd (Castle Acres, Narborough, Leicester LE19 1BY): title page, pp. 31 (bottom), 33 (top), 57 (bottom), 79 (bottom), 128 (bottom), 134 (bottom); Felinfoel Brewery Co Ltd (Farmers Row, Felinfoel, Llanelli, Dyfed SA14 8LB): pp. 44 (top), 56 (top), 93, 94 (top); Fuller, Smith & Turner plc (The Griffin Brewery, Chiswick, London W4 2QB): pp. 37 (bottom), 51 (bottom), 69 (top); Greene King plc (Westgate Brewery, Bury St Edmunds, Suffolk IP33 1QT): pp. 19 (top), 32 (bottom), 41, 45 (top), 88, 89; Hardys & Hansons plc (The Brewery, Kimberley, Nottingham NG16 2NS): pp. 22 (top), 26 (bottom), 39 (top), 86, 139 (bottom); Harvey & Sons (Lewes) Ltd (Bridge Wharf Brewery, 6 Cliffe High Street, Lewes, East Sussex BN7 2AH): pp. 55, 73 (bottom); Interbrew UK Ltd (Tennent's Wellpark Brewery, 161 Duke Street, Glasgow G31 1JD): pp. 44 (bottom), 119, 120–1, 122; Jennings Brothers plc (Castle Brewery, Cockermouth, Cumbra CA13 9NE): pp. 10, 22 (bottom), 23 (bottom), 27 (bottom), 35 (top), 38 (top), 52, 53 (bottom), 62 (top), 104; George Newman: pp. 46, 62 (bottom), 102 (bottom); T.D. Ridley & Sons Ltd (Hartford End Brewery, Chelmsford, Essex CM3 1JZ): p. 72 (top); Frederick Robinson Ltd, Unicorn Brewery, Stockport, Cheshire SK1 1JJ): pp. 6, 47, 58–9, 63, 90, 91, 92, 103 (bottom), 126–7, 134 (top), 136; St Austell Brewery company Ltd (63 Trevarthian Road, St Austell, Cornwall PL25 4BY): pp. 18, 34 (top), 51 (top), 76 (bottom), 132 (bottom); Scottish & Newcastle plc (33 Ellersly Road, Edinburgh EH12 6HX): pp. 8, 9, 35 (bottom), 36 (bottom), 37 (top), 57 (top), 100 (top), 112–13; Scottish Brewing Archive (University of Glasgow, 13 Thurso Street, Glasgow G11 6PE): pp. 44 (bottom), 107, 108–9, 112, 113, 114, 116–17, 118 (top), 119, 120–1, 122; Shepherd Neame Ltd (Faversham Brewery, 17 Court Street, Faversham, Kent ME13 7AX): pp. 19 (bottom), 24, 28, 31 (top), 40 (top), 45 (bottom), 53 (top), 74, 128 (top), 129; David Smith: pp. 3, 4, 5, 30 (bottom), 80, 81, 82 (top), 83, 84; Traquair House Brewery Ltd (Traquair House, Innerleithen, Peebleshire EH44 6PW): pp. 97, 106 (bottom); Steve Wilson: pp. 15, 25 (bottom), 27 (top), 30 (top); York Brewery Co Ltd (12 Toft Green, Micklegate, York YO1 6JT): pp. 7, 100 (bottom), 139 (top);Young & Co's Brewery plc (The Ram Brewery, Wandsworth, London SW18 4JD): pp. 25 (top), 26 (top), 29, 33 (bottom), 49, 54, 66, 69 (bottom), 70.

INDEX